DESIGNED BY GOD

DESIGNED BY GOD

*Honest Talk About Beauty,
Modesty, and Self-Image*

REGINA FRANKLIN

Discovery House Publishers

Books, music, and videos that feed the soul with the Word of God

Box 3566 Grand Rapids, MI 49501

Discovery House Publishers is affiliated with RBC Ministries,
Grand Rapids, Michigan.

Discovery House books are distributed to the trade exclusively by
Barbour Publishing, Inc., Uhrichsville, Ohio.

Requests for permission to quote from this book should be directed to:
Permissions Department, Discovery House Publishers,
P.O. Box 3566, Grand Rapids, MI 49501.

Unless otherwise indicated, Scripture quotations are from the New
International Version © 1973, 1978, 1984 by International Bible Society.
Used by permission of Zondervan Bible Publishers. All rights reserved.

Portions of this book have been excerpted and/or adapted from
Who Calls Me Beautiful? by Regina Franklin,
published by Discovery House Publishers.

Portions of chapter four were excerpted and adapted from
"Not Outerwear." *Soul Journey: Meditations on God's Leading Through Life.*
Summer 2005.

Names and certain details have been changed to protect people's privacy.

Library of Congress Cataloging-in-Publication Data
Franklin, Regina.
    Designed by God : honest talk about beauty, modesty, and self-image /
Regina Franklin.
        p. cm.
    Includes bibliographical references.
    ISBN 1-57293-174-4
    1. Women--Religious life. 2. Self-perception--Religious aspects--
Christianity. 3. Body, Human--Religious aspects--Christianity. 4. Beauty,
Personal. 5. Modesty--Religious aspects--Christianity. I. Title.
    BV4527.F734 2006
    248.8'43--dc22
                                                                2006028674

Printed in the United States of America

06 07 08 09 / DP / 10 9 8 7 6 5 4 3 2 1

*To the women who labor with me in youth ministry
and to the young women who give us the honor
of pouring our lives into theirs*

Contents

.1

BEAUTY AND THE DECEPTION

EMILY walks uncertainly down the school hallway with its pale blue walls and well-worn linoleum. Early morning chatter fills the corridor, but she does not participate. Instead she pastes a smile on her face to match the look of assurance she sees on those around her. She adjusts her heavy backpack, but it does not ease the heaviness in her heart.

At her locker, she begins her morning ritual. The plastic mirror inside draws her attention past the pink flower border and into the eyes staring back at her. Fluorescent lights cast a pale tinge on her reflection. Thanks to the meticulous use of a hairdryer, curling iron, gel, and spray, her hair appears to fall naturally around her face. She brushes it aside to inspect the carefully applied makeup that she depends on to hide her doubt.

She rehearses her smile as she has done so many times before—in front of the bathroom mirror, storefront windows, even the rearview mirror of her car—until it matches the look she sees in magazines. Eyes wide open, teeth held apart, smile lightly parted. To her, beauty means effort.

GOD'S WORD SAYS

Do not love the world nor the things in the world. If anyone loves the world, the love of the Father is not in him. For all that is in the world, the lust of the flesh and the lust of the eyes and the boastful pride of life, is not from the Father, but is from the world. The world is passing away, and also its lusts; but the one who does the will of God lives forever. —1 John 2:15-17 NASB

The harsh sound of the warning bell reverberates in her ears. She reaches into her purse for the necklace and earrings she grabbed off her dresser in her morning rush. She puts them on, adjusts her shirt and jeans, and takes one last look in the mirror. Slamming her locker door shut and turning to face her day, she feels a sea of eyes staring back at her. She searches for any sign of approval. Though she tries hard to appear natural, she feels posed like a Barbie doll.

What do they see? Do they like me? her heart asks. *Do they think I am beautiful?*

Growing up isn't easy. Makeup, clothes, accessories, diets, exercise. And plenty of tears—the kind that make your mascara run. Deep down you wonder, *Is there nothing more to being a girl than worrying about how you look?*

As a little girl, Emily never questioned her beauty. She enjoyed watching herself dance in front of the mirror. She would study her reflection, smile, twirl, and make a funny face. But somewhere along the way, the little girl became a young woman who is no longer certain of her beauty.

She's not the only one.

Every girl wants to know she's beautiful. Yet each one, at some point, loses touch with the confident little girl within. Instead of smiling at the image in the mirror, she begins to use the world as her mirror. Unable to measure up to the images of perfect people, she becomes dissatisfied with how she looks.

When I was young, beauty pageants mesmerized me. Scanning the TV guide, I looked forward to watching the three big pageants: Miss America, Miss USA, and Miss Universe. I imagined myself dancing and singing like the contestants, and I longed to be one of them.

The women onstage epitomized poise and grace. Dressed in sophisticated gowns, high-heeled shoes, and glittering jewelry, they seemed to have the world at their fingertips. I chose my favorite and became caught up in the drama. If she won, I won.

THE WORLD SAYS

- "Get a toned body in two weeks"[1]

- "Make Over Your Body: Exercises that can make you look taller and leaner in time for school"[2]

- "Pretty, Easy Makeup: Look gorgeous—fast!"[3]

- "Almost famous: Four young models on the verge prove how easy it can bo to change your look"[4]

- "The best-dressed girls in America: Four of *Seventeen*'s 'best-dressed' girls in America posed for our camera in their Aeropostale denim 'must-haves' for back-to-school."[5]

Very few young women win the title and wear the crown, but all compete—with other girls in the lunchroom, at the mall, or even at church. You know the feeling. It's like being in a contest but not being sure of the categories or how to earn points. Beauty becomes a game of trying to discover what others seem to have found, but which continually eludes your grasp.

Whether you're online chatting with friends, reading a magazine, or watching your favorite television show, you see a steady stream of guarantees promising a newer, prettier you—if only you find the perfect look, lose ten pounds, buy designer clothes, or use certain products.

Hair products will give you curls or remove the curls you've always hated. Skin products will remove bumps or spots that keep your face from glowing perfection. Makeup will make your lashes longer, your eyes bigger, and your lips fuller.

The real message: You aren't good enough.

Is it any wonder that girls are unhappy with who they are?

God never intended for us to feel broken. He never intended for us to struggle to be beautiful. He never intended for us to question our value and worth. These thoughts and feelings come from living in a broken world. Instead of learning God's definition of beauty, we unthinkingly accept the world's definition and take on its brokenness in the process. We're being deceived, and we've lived with the lie for so long that we can't see the truth.

We trade away true beauty, which improves with age and lasts forever, and we're left with an endless search for physical perfection and a broken heart when we find out how soon "false" beauty fades.

God designed you for beauty, so desiring it is not sinful. But

He desires to give you much more than the world has to offer. He longs to take away the ache in your heart. He longs for you to know how beautiful you are.

Thankfully, God's Word tells us how our understanding of beauty has been broken and also how to restore our understanding of His original design.

The apostle John, one of the New Testament writers, mentions three ways that the world corrupts our understanding of beauty. They are the lust of the flesh, the lust of the eyes, and the boastful pride of life (1 John 2:16).

Beauty Brings Satisfaction

When we hear the word *lust* we usually think of sexual desire, but it involves much more than that. To lust is to desire something so intensely that the desire controls you.

Teen magazines intensify lust by focusing on skin and flesh. They address the longing for beauty by exaggerating the importance of appearance. Images of physically perfect young women dominate advertisements. Advertisers know that before you will buy their product, you must feel a need for it. So they try to create desire for what they are selling. To do so, they use images of women who fit society's definition of beauty. The message? Satisfaction is attained only by achieving their standard of beauty.

You begin to believe what they are saying—that your desire for beauty can be satisfied by what you see in the picture. Beauty then becomes linked not only with the product but with satisfaction.

Copying the hairstyles and fashions of stars seems harmless, yet these habits take you in the wrong direction. You walk away believing that you have to look a particular way to be content with who you are. You doubt that you have what it takes to be beautiful.

Because the enemy of God is out to destroy God's design for your life, he wants you to believe that the image the world offers can satisfy your God-given longing for beauty. It's the same old lie from the Garden of Eden. One of the reasons Eve took the forbidden fruit and ate it was that she saw it "was good for food" (Genesis 3:6). The enemy deceived her into thinking the fruit could satisfy her longings.

God's enemy does the same to you when he convinces you that the only way to be satisfied is to reflect popular images of beauty. Physical beauty looks good; it looks satisfying. But it cannot satisfy you any more than the fruit could satisfy Eve.

God created your longing for beauty to draw you into a closer relationship with Him. But His enemy takes what He designed for your good and uses it against you. Eventually, you begin to think the desires of your flesh are more real than God's love for you. When you try to satisfy these longings apart from God, you become ruled by lust rather than by the Spirit of God. You wind up feeling emptier than before your search began. When your love for the world separates you from the heart of God—rather than your love for God separating you from the world—Satan is accomplishing what he set out to do.

Beauty Brings Acceptance

The desire for acceptance has a great deal to do with our eyes. While the eyes can be a powerful way of engaging God's world, they can also pull us into a love affair with the world instead of with God. This is called "the lust of the eyes" (1 John 2:16).

Because our eyes are the primary way we interact with our world, what we see sometimes ignites a passion for things that are not of God.

Furthermore, our eyes are the primary way the world interacts with us. You may have heard the saying, "Eyes are the window to the soul." Regardless of the expression on your face, much of what you are thinking or feeling can be read in your eyes.

> ## THE WORLD SAYS
>
> "Hair Help: Use these products, and your guy won't be able to resist running his fingers through your hair"[10]
>
> "Sultry and Seductive on the inside, luminous brunette on the outside" (advertisement for hair care)[11]

When I was a resident assistant in college, a girl on my floor was known for putting on a happy face even when she was having a really bad day. When I asked her how she was doing, she would usually say, "Fine," with a big smile. Sometimes, though, I would tell her, "That's not true because your eyes say otherwise." No matter how hard she tried to hide her feelings behind her smile, her eyes would give her away. Eyes reveal a lot about how we're really feeling.

So how does this apply to beauty?

Like everyone, you want acceptance. And in your search for it, you allow the eyes of others to determine how you see yourself.

Cut, copy, paste. Today's technology enables you to remake almost anything into the image of your dreams. No more need for scissors to remove anything unwanted from a photo. Simply scan the picture, crop out unwanted parts, and paste in something new.

While this technology is both fascinating and convenient, it creates the expectation of perfection. Real life doesn't cut, copy, and paste.

We wonder why we don't measure up to the air-brushed, digitalized pictures we see when what we're seeing isn't even real.

When makeup, hair color, and dieting fail to produce perfection in us, we turn to more drastic measures. Whatever it takes to find "the look." Whatever it takes to get noticed.

More and more girls see plastic surgery and botox as the answer to low self-esteem. A cut-and-paste body in a cut-and-paste world.

God does not want digitalized reproductions. He wants a relationship with a real person. Are we willing to be real with Him?

You begin looking into their eyes to find out how they see you. Knowing that others are watching you keeps you focused on getting and keeping their attention. All for the sake of finding acceptance.

God made us to desire acceptance from Him, not the world. Here again, Satan takes a God-given desire and perverts it to confuse us.

Just as Eve saw that the fruit was "pleasing to the eye," we want to know that we are pleasing to the eyes of this world. Consumed with a lust for approval, we turn away from the most complete and pure acceptance we could ever know . . . God's.

Beauty Brings Power

No one wants to feel powerless. So it's not surprising that every girl wants to feel as if she has some measure of control over her life. Sometimes that desire can be as simple as proving that she's got life together. But the desire, if not managed in the right way, can quickly become the "boastful pride of life."

Girl power is no passing fad. While it's important for girls to be able to make choices for their own lives (within certain parameters, such as love for God and respect for parents), the message of girl power has hidden dangers. Movies, music videos, and images of women in general tell us that power belongs only to those who are beautiful.

Sometimes the message takes the form of physical power. The portrayal of women in action films celebrates females who are physically aggressive. Images of women beating up men, and women beating up other women, show us a world that values women who physically dominate others. Often the women are either barely dressed or dressed in tight clothing. The provocative look combined with physical aggression works to destroy God's plan for a woman's sexuality and her beauty.

Young women want the confidence of being able to overcome whatever or whoever stands in their way. This makes them susceptible to the "pride of life" temptation which says that power comes from physical perfection or sexual attraction.

Most girls however are not looking to give someone "a beat down." We're happy to settle for emotional power. We know we can buy a great looking outfit that will get people's attention and help us gain their acceptance. Once that happens we're much more likely to get what we want from them. We use our looks to control other people's emotions. Wanting to be "in the know," we buy into the lie that if we can control others' responses we have proven our worth.

Knowing you have the ability to control emotions by the way

you look is an exciting and powerful feeling, but it's a dangerous kind of power that needs to be used with caution.

Eve ate the forbidden fruit because she fell for Satan's lie—that he can give us what belongs to God: beauty, wisdom, and power. But all of Satan's substitutes fail to deliver on their promises.

Looking in the Mirror

1. Give three examples of advertisements that use a woman's face or body to sell products. What promises do these products make? How likely is it that the product can fulfill such a promise?

2. How do these images affect how you feel about yourself?

3. How does the desire for control affect a girl's relationships with guys? What messages is society sending to guys (through movies, advertisements, etc.) about a girl's value?

4. How do these messages affect how guys treat girls?

5. Have you ever used your body to gain approval from others? In what ways?

6. Read John 8:44. What does this Scripture teach us about our enemy?

7. Knowing that God desires to give us His beauty, how should we look at the images in magazines, music videos, and movies that perpetuate the world's idea of ideal beauty?

Show me your ways, O Lord, teach me your paths; guide me in

your truth and teach me, for you are God my Savior,

and my hope is in you all day long.

–Psalm 25:4-5

..2

Voices All Around

WHEN I was twelve years old my family moved from a small town in Minnesota to a suburb of Minneapolis. I went from having a wide circle of friends to knowing no one. I was lonely, unsure, and feeling the need for acceptance.

A girl in the church youth group had the kind of acceptance I longed for. Everybody liked her. The guys wanted to date her, and the girls wanted to *be* her. Even adults sought her attention. She represented the standard of beauty that the rest of us tried to achieve—tall, blond, and confident. I was short, awkward, and insecure. She lived in the world of the beautiful; I did not. I saw her as the key to making it "in." I thought I had to change myself, so I tried to look like her.

Even to the point of stupidity.

I do not tan easily, but I have no problem getting a great burn. One Saturday I went with her and some other girls to the lake.

Their tanned skin looked great, so when they passed around the baby oil, I set aside my sunscreen and convinced myself that the baby oil would keep me from burning. By the time I got home, I looked like a boiled lobster, and I was as miserable on the inside as I was on the outside.

But even that experience didn't give me a clue that being *like* someone else wouldn't *make* me a somebody. Instead I tried new ways to achieve the beauty that seemed so natural to her.

One Sunday when I was fourteen, I stood with her in the foyer after church. I had finally reached the age where I was allowed to wear makeup, and I talked excitedly about the new products I had purchased.

After my exuberant announcement, she casually asked, "Have you thought about trying brown eyeliner instead of blue?"

She didn't intend to hurt me, but I was devastated by her comment. It reminded me that I still didn't measure up.

I looked up to her for all the wrong reasons. I was created to be uniquely me, not her. I know now that her approval would not have made me love myself—nor would the approval of anyone else. But it was a long time before I saw the truth about how broken I was on the inside.

And I now wonder how she felt about herself. She was constantly trying to lose weight. When she won a modeling contest, the judge told her she needed to lose ten pounds before the photo shoot. I would have given anything for her body, but even she wasn't good enough for the world. I never questioned whether she loved herself. I just assumed she did because I saw her as perfect.

I've talked to countless girls who, to me, have the "perfect look" but who still hate the way they look. While other girls look at them as the standard of beauty, they think they're not beautiful enough.

Every girl wants approval. It's a hard but unavoidable truth. Others' opinions matter. You want to know what others think about you. And you want it to be positive.

The need for approval is complicated. We come into this world wanting to be loved. And we equate approval with love. But the search for approval can keep us from finding love because it leads us away from the One who truly loves us and who created us to be one-of-a-kind.

Our lives are stories in the making. Each day we write another page. Our favorite stories end with the villains being defeated and the heroine rescued. We want the same ending for our own lives. But too often we let others do the dictating. In listening to the voices of others and seeking their approval, we are trusting them to write a happy ending.

Voices of Peers

Peer pressure is an inescapable reality. From the clothes you buy to the things you do, your decisions are significantly affected by your friends. According to one girl,

> There are those who don't care what anyone has to say about what they wear, those who care what everyone has to say about what they wear, and then there is *"everyone,"* the group of people that seem to set the standards by which *"everyone that is anyone"* must follow[1] (emphasis added).

So who is everyone? And why do we care so much what *everyone* thinks? The answer is clear: "A lot of people are afraid of rejection."[2]

Leah doesn't want to feel left out. To secure her place among her peers, she dresses like her friends, listens to the same music, and even talks like them. To gain acceptance, she loses her own identity.

Megan on the other hand lets those she doesn't even like influence her decisions. She intentionally acts and dresses the opposite of everyone around her. She convinces herself that she's an individual, but she's really isolating herself so she doesn't have to risk being rejected. She too is allowing others to control her decisions and shape her self-worth.

Voices of Family

Families should be a place of belonging, a place of safety. That is what God intended. However, even well-meaning family members can adversely affect the way we see ourselves. Words never intended to hurt us ring in our ears long after they are spoken. Sometimes the words are so painful we have trouble forgetting.

My family didn't live close to our extended family, but my sister and I enjoyed going to visit them. Along with the good memories, though, I always returned home with a few new negative voices in my mind, usually related to the shape and size of my hips.

Large hips are one of the defining features of the women in our family. Looking at me and shaking their heads, family members would say, "Uh-huh, you've got your grandmomma's hips." I knew these words were no compliment because my grandmother did not see herself as beautiful. So when I was told I had hips like hers it was as if I was being told that I was defective, marked for life by the size of my hips.

Scripture says that the power of life and death is in the tongue (Proverbs 18:21) and that "A word aptly spoken is like apples of gold in settings of silver" (Proverbs 25:11). Just as gold and silver are precious elements, so too is a right word spoken at the right time in the right way.

The things family members say to one another are not always *aptly spoken*. Families "tell each other like it is," and the conversations often include sarcasm and relentless teasing. For some reason, we think this kidding is a way of showing love for one another. But negative words do not communicate love, even when we claim we're just kidding. While it is true that families need to joke and have fun, when laughter comes at the expense of someone's sense of worth, the joke is not funny.

I know my extended family loved me, but they had grown accustomed to cutting one another down with words. It was the way they related to each other. In their eyes, they were "just teasing" and showing me they loved me enough to pick on me. They never intended for their words to hurt me. But to me, their teasing meant much more, and their comments did hurt. Their comments echoed the doubts I had about my beauty and worth, and their words became a part of my story.

In some cases, the voices we hear are negative words others speak about themselves.

My parents always told me to try my best. They didn't push me to excel. Their expectation was simply to try my best at whatever was before me.

While both parents encouraged me, my dad taught me to dream. Although he died of cancer shortly before his fifty-first birthday, he was one of the most influential people in my life. The most important thing I learned from him was that to love God is to desire to know Him more.

However, my father taught me something he never intended for me to learn.

Despite my father's many accomplishments, he was always frustrated with his physical appearance, especially his weight. He was always on a diet. Whether he was counting calories, stocking the fridge with diet foods, or buying new exercise stuff, my dad was in a never-ending cycle to change his appearance. While there is nothing wrong with wanting to be healthy, my dad was looking to change himself on the outside so he could feel good about himself on the inside.

He, too, heard voices around him. He saw that society based a man's worth on his appearance. Even as a pastor, my dad battled the expectations of others. Although most people valued his genuine love for others, he focused on his inadequacies. He assumed people wanted him to be someone other than who he was.

Even his achievements could not make the voices go away. While my father was a talented musician, a gifted teacher, and a trustworthy man, he lost sight of what made him truly valuable. My dad struggled to love himself as the man God had created him to be.

And so the voices he heard became the voices he spoke.

Dad was infamous for saying, "Do as I say, not as I do." He usually said this after we caught him doing something he had told us not to do—like leaving a mess in the kitchen or driving ten miles an hour over the speed limit. But what a parent *does* carries just as much of an impact as what a parent *says*. So even though my father made it clear to me that I was not to cut myself down, his words about himself sent another message.

I grew up hearing my dad talk negatively about himself, so I thought it was okay to speak the same way about myself. My dad never told me that I was fat, that I could never do anything right, or that I was a failure. So it wasn't his words about me that influenced my self-perception. But I heard my dad speak these words about himself. And his words became a part of me.

I chose to believe I didn't measure up. I chose to believe the world's message about physical appearance. I chose to believe I wasn't beautiful.

Living Beyond the Voices

She lived in a story created from others' opinions. Looking for someone to love her, she made choices that isolated her from the other women. Knowing what they thought of her, she stayed far outside their circles of conversation and activity.

Carrying the empty pitcher to the well, she was alone as usual. Alone in her thoughts, alone in her hurts. Most of the women had already been to the well to gather water in the cool of the day. Going later kept her safe from their comments. Or so she thought. In truth, she lived in the shadow of their opinions.

As she walked the path from her home to the well, she probably thought this day would be like every other—confusing, painful, and lonely. After all, she didn't belong. Her parched soul, as dry and empty as the water pitcher she carried, longed to know that she was worth loving. Believing the lie that having a man would make her feel loved, she had tried to fill the emptiness with one relationship after another. But nothing could satisfy.

Until that day.

In John 4 we read the story of Jesus' encounter with the woman at the well. Scripture doesn't tell us her thoughts, but I wonder if she cringed when she saw someone waiting by the well. Did she wonder what He would think of her? Was she afraid of what He might say to her? Was she hoping and yet dreading that He would overlook her as the others did? She knew the voice of rejection all too well. Man after man had entered her life and left. To make matters worse, she was hated by Jews because of her ancestry.

Most Jews walked right past her because they considered Samaritans unworthy of their time and attention. She had heard the labels others had placed on her, and now those labels were the very ones she used to define herself. So when Jesus asked her for a drink of water, she was taken aback. "You are a Jew and I am a Samaritan woman. How can you ask me for a drink?" she asked (John 4:9).

Rather than be offended by her question, Jesus gently told her, "If you knew the gift of God and who it is that asks you for a drink, you would have asked him and he would have given you living water" (John 4:10).

He knew what she wanted most, and He knew that the story she was living in was not the one He had written for her.

We, too, want to know we have value and worth but feel trapped by the voices we hear. Confused by what we hear and wanting others' approval, we look for the answers to our questions in the world around us. Society's messages, peer pressure, and family hurts go a long way in shaping how we feel about ourselves.

Caught up in the opinions of others, we forget we are created, loved, and chosen.

We push ourselves to become physically perfect like other girls who seem to have it all together. Maybe if we look beautiful enough, we tell ourselves, then others will love and accept us. Trying to satisfy our thirst for belonging, we mold ourselves according to the world's image of beauty. We try to change ourselves on the outside so we can love who we are on the inside.

But we pay a high price. Confused and uncertain, we end up living in a story that isn't ours. Most of all, we miss seeing that everything we've ever desired stands right in front of us.

God knows your story. He knows the young woman He created you to be.

But God cannot unfold His plans for us if we're too busy

GOD'S WORD SAYS

"For I know the plans I have for you," declares the LORD, "plans to prosper you and not to harm you, plans to give you hope and a future." —Jeremiah 29:11

trying to be somebody we're not. He cannot show us the wonderful thoughts He has toward us if we're too busy listening to other voices. He cannot heal our shattered self-worth if we're too busy holding on to the painful things others have said about us.

When we let Him heal us, He will show us how to hear words of love instead of words of failure. We will exalt God rather than the opinions of others. And eventually we will live by His love instead of our brokenness.

Looking in the Mirror

1. On a scale of 1 to 10 (with 1 being not much at all and 10 being a lot), how much do your friends' opinions influence you?

2. Have your peers ever said anything to you that has made you feel as if you didn't have value? If so, how have those words shaped how you feel about yourself, and how have those words affected the decisions you've made?

3. How have the things your family has said to you influenced how you feel about yourself?

4. What other voices have you heard?

5. What does Proverbs 16:24 say about the power of words?

6. Read Proverbs 12:18.

- What words have cut you like the "thrust of a sword"?

- What people have spoken words of healing (words of encouragement or affirmation)?

7. Why must we forgive those who have hurt us with their words?

8. Explain what the following verses say about forgiveness.
    Psalm 86:5
    Mark 11:26
    Luke 6:36-38

9. Take a moment to think about the words that come out of your mouth (either about yourself or about others). Do you speak words that heal or words that cut?

10. Here are some additional Scriptures to study regarding the power of our words:
    Colossians 4:6
    2 Timothy 1:13

When your words came, I ate them; they were my joy and my heart's delight, for I bear your name, O Lord God Almighty.

–Jeremiah 15:16

...3

TRUE BEAUTY

ITH her head tucked down and her arms at her side, she
walks up to the building she knows so well. Her pockets are
filled with rocks, and their heaviness matches the heaviness of
her heart. The cross at the top of the roof quietly reaches toward
her. Peace. The strong, pierced hands sculpted into the door
invite her to enter. Safety. The communion cup and bread on
the table gently whisper her name. Belonging. She steps inside.
Sanctuary.

Slowly she lifts her head and looks around. She reaches into
her pocket and grasps one of the rocks. Its jagged edges press
painfully into her skin. Approaching the altar, she turns to look
out the nearest window. Even the beauty of the sunlight streaming
through the windows cannot stop the tears from running down her
cheeks.

I hate myself. Her piercing shriek echoes off the wall

accompanied by the sound of shattering glass as she hurls the rock through the window. *I will never fit in.* Another rock leaves her hand, and another window shatters. *I will never measure up.* The cup and the bread tumble to the floor with the fury of her pain. *I am so ugly.* Rock after rock. The shattered windows and spilled communion cup lie around her. Her heart is broken. Gone is peace. Gone is safety. Gone is belonging. Slumped on her knees, she weeps over the brokenness, the loss of sanctuary.

Hearing the buzz of her alarm, Angela reluctantly climbs from her bed and heads toward the bathroom. Leaning over the sink, she splashes cold water on her face. As she lifts her head, she sees herself in the mirror. *Ugh, I look terrible.* She avoids the mirror as she steps into the shower. *My thighs are so huge.* As she dries her body, she moves to her closet and flips through her clothes. She grabs one item only to replace it with another. *Nothing ever looks good on me.* After finally choosing an outfit, she finishes her morning routine. *My hair is hopeless.* Word after word, rock after rock. Her heart hears the shattering of glass.

She feels broken but cannot figure out why. At school and even at church she feels absolutely alone. She tries to pray but doesn't get the response everyone at church talks about. She looks at the faces smiling around her—girls laughing at a shared joke, families spending time together, a boyfriend and girlfriend holding hands—and thinks she'll never find a place where she truly belongs.

God wants us to find our sanctuary in Him. He longs to wrap His arms around us and pull us close to Him. He longs to be our "place of refuge and protection."[1] He longs to be the place where we discover beauty.

Fearfully and Wonderfully Made

Psalm 139 expresses how intimately God knows us—down to the tiniest detail.

Sadly, we seldom feel "fearfully and wonderfully made." Instead we keep a list of everything we wish we could change about ourselves. We're quick to remind God, "My nose is too big, my thighs are too fat, and my hair is boring." How could something created with care turn out so ugly and imperfect?

His heart holds the answer.

> ## GOD'S WORD SAYS
>
> For you created my inmost being; you knit me together in my mother's womb. I praise you because I am fearfully and wonderfully made; your works are wonderful, I know that full well.
> —Psalm 139:13-14

You were formed by God. He didn't just watch from a distance when you were created: "Before I formed you in the womb I knew you; before you were born I set you apart" (Jeremiah 1:5). When God looks at you, He doesn't see short legs, a big nose, or unruly hair. He sees the artistic wonder of His hands.

Furthermore, His interest in you didn't stop with your creation. To Him, you are priceless, and He wants to be with you. No matter who rejects you, God does not. He wants you to be just who He created you to be, not anyone else.

Your amazing body and unique personality tell of the creative power of God. You were created in His very image (Genesis 1:27). Therefore, when God looks at you, He sees something of Himself. You are indeed a wonder.

Paying the Price

The world will tell you that it pays to be beautiful, and also that beauty will cost you. They are partly right. True beauty does demand a price. But they are wrong in expecting you to pay it. The bill has already been paid; true beauty is yours to receive.

The apostle John wrote, "For God so loved the world that he gave his one and only Son, that whoever believes in him shall not perish but have eternal life" (John 3:16). This verse seems to have little to do with beauty, but we must remember that true beauty is not what we see on the covers of *Seventeen* and *Teen Vogue*.

When we accept Jesus as Savior and Lord, the Spirit of God comes to live inside us. The apostle Paul reminded believers living in the Roman city of Corinth that they were God's temple, and that the Holy Spirit lived in them (1 Corinthians 3:16).

When God looks at you, He not only sees that you were created out of His great love, He also sees His Spirit living in you. He sees His own beauty ready to blossom in you.

The prophet Isaiah said Jesus would have "no beauty or majesty to attract us to him, nothing in his appearance that we should desire him" (Isaiah 53:2). The world looked at Jesus and saw no worth because its understanding of beauty is superficial. When our definition of beauty matches that of the world, we too miss seeing His true beauty.

In the greatest display of beauty ever, God offered His own Son to be the sacrifice for our sin. He died so that we could have true beauty. "For the LORD takes pleasure in His people; He will beautify the humble with salvation" (Psalm 149:4 NKJV). Salvation heals our brokenness. It removes the ugly sin and replaces it with the likeness of Christ, a beauty that goes much deeper than our skin.

Every time I long to look like the model on a magazine cover, I am saying that artificial beauty is better than the true beauty reclaimed by God with the blood of His Son.

Choosing Christ is not just a decision I make in order to have eternal life. It is a decision that changes every part of my life, including the way I see beauty.

Do you want the beauty of this world or the beauty of Christ? If you want to be the temple of the Holy Spirit, the choice is clear.

GOD'S WORD SAYS

Do you not know that your body is a temple of the Holy Spirit, who is in you, whom you have received from God? You are not your own; you were bought at a price. Therefore honor God with your body. —1 Corinthians 6:19-20

Dying to Self

We talk about "falling in love" or "love at first sight," but neither phrase accurately describes the amazing phenomenon that turns our world upside down. We are quick to associate warm, positive feelings with love. While those emotions might be an aspect of love, they are not the whole thing. Love is more than feeling.

I remember the night my husband first told me he loved me. As we stood out in my parents' front yard, he took my hands in his and said, "There's something important I have to tell you." When he said those words, I knew what was coming. Scott had made a commitment to say "I love you" only to the girl he intended to marry.

In that moment I knew I had a choice to make. Although I felt incredible being with him, and my feelings toward him grew stronger every day, loving him was still a choice. I understood that Scott had counted the cost of what it would mean to love me, and I had to count the cost as well. To say that I loved him would mean that I was willing to commit the rest of my life to him in marriage. It would mean that I was going to forsake all others to choose him.

We generally think of love in terms of what it will bring us, not what it will cost us. But love means sacrifice.

GOD'S WORD SAYS

Therefore, I urge you, brothers, in view of God's mercy, to offer your bodies as living sacrifices, holy and pleasing to God—this is your spiritual act of worship. —Romans 12:1

The word *sacrifice* is the Greek word *thusia* and it comes from the word *thuo,* which means "to slay, [or] to kill."[2] When a sacrifice takes place, something dies. Jesus demonstrated the sacrificial nature of love when He died for us, but our love for Him requires a death as well. Loving God means I must die to myself.

God's willingness to give His Son to die for us proves how much He loves us. But it's not enough simply to acknowledge that love; we have to make a choice about what to do with it. He stands, holding our hands in His, declaring His love for us (Jeremiah 31:3). To love Him is to choose Him above all else.

"Dying to self" is a phrase we often talk about in church. But what does it mean? By nature, people are selfish. We want things to go our way. We have our plans, our dreams, our desires. The world draws us in by promising that we'll get what we want if we follow its advice. Dying to self means being willing to let go of having things our way in order to do things God's way. It means wanting Him more than anything else.

When asked to name the greatest commandment, "Jesus replied, 'Love the Lord your God with all your heart and with all your soul and with all your mind. This is the first and greatest commandment" (Matthew 22:37-38).

If I love God with all of my being, I will see all of my being through His love. To love Him is to let go of my desire for worldliness—including the kind of beauty the world values. When I do, I no longer define myself, or others, as the world does. I have made a commitment—a life choice—to love Him above all else.

To determine whether your heart longs for the beauty of this world or the beauty of Christ, ask yourself these questions:

- Do I care more about my physical appearance than my relationship with God?
- Do I spend more time in front of the mirror than I do talking to God?
- Do I look forward to reading the Word of God as much as I do the latest fashion magazines?
- Do I spend more time wanting to look like movie stars or cover models or wanting to look like Christ?
- Do I place more importance on having friends who fit the world's standard of beauty or God's?

God longs for our devotion. But we cannot be devoted to two masters. We cannot say we love God above all else while giving all of our attention to the world. Our hearts must be undivided (Ezekiel 11:19-20).

God promises to renew our hearts so we can love Him to the fullest. He wants to remove the "stony heart" that desires the world's beauty and give us a "new heart" that wants true beauty.

In Psalm 37 we read, "Delight yourself in the LORD and he will give you the desires of your heart" (v. 4). This Scripture doesn't mean that if we delight in God, He will grant our desire to look like our favorite celebrity. Instead, it teaches that when we delight in the Lord, He will change the desires of our heart—we'll begin to want what He wants. Rather than wanting to look like the girl on the magazine cover, we will want to look like Christ.

For a long time I prayed that God would change the way I looked so I could learn to love myself. I asked God to help me diet, to find the right clothes, make me anyone but me. I had it all wrong. It was my heart, not my body, that needed to change.

But I had never asked Him to change my heart.

Arriving home from church one Sunday, I went straight to my bedroom. I was lonely and I hated myself. Most of all I was tired of feeling as if I could never measure up. Still in my church clothes, I curled up on the bed and began to cry. Over the years I had cried a lot of tears over the way I looked. But this time the tears were different—they were deeper. I begged God to change me—not on the outside, but on the inside. Saying the words aloud for the first time, I told God that I hated my body and I hated myself, but I didn't want to continue hating myself. I wanted to stop chasing the shadow of beauty that the world said I needed to have. I asked God to show me the beauty He saw in me. I asked Him to show me the beauty that Christ paid for with His life.

On that day, I stopped asking God to make me thin and beautiful. And since then I've been discovering that true beauty comes not from how I look but from the depths of who I am.

I want my body, my mind, my heart—every part of me—to be a sacrifice to the Lord because I love Him. I make my life a sacrifice not because I *have* to love Him but because I *choose* to. Every day, I choose to love Him above all else.

To become the beautiful woman God created me to be I must first give everything to the One who created me. Learning to be deeply in love with Jesus means dying to myself and to this world.

Jesus loved you enough to die so you could be free from worldly standards. Finding your beauty in Christ means saying, "I have been crucified with Christ and I no longer live, but Christ lives in me. The life I live in the body, I live by faith in the Son of God, who loved me and gave himself for me" (Galatians 2:20).

You will no longer feel compelled to wear what others say is "in." You will no longer be depressed if your hair doesn't look as if you just stepped off a photo shoot. You will no longer panic if your makeup doesn't cover every flaw. You will no longer obsess over being as thin as the currently popular celebrity.

When you begin to comprehend the significance of being the temple of the living God, your old view of beauty will shrivel up and die.

Every girl longs to know true peace, safety, and belonging. In Christ, all these become possible. When you choose to love Him above all else, not only do you find the greatest love you could ever know, you also find your sanctuary.

Looking in the Mirror

1. Does the way you think about yourself reveal that you care more about what the world says or about what God says?

2. Take a moment to think about places in your life where you still struggle with insecurities about your worth. Identify some of these areas. What hinders you from seeing your beauty in Christ?

3. What desires of your heart need to change?

4. Do certain things about your physical appearance "have" to be a certain way in order for you to feel beautiful? How must you "die to self" in regard to these areas?

5. The apostle Paul wrote the following words to describe the freedom we have in Christ: "But now that you know God—or rather are known by God—how is it that you are turning back to those weak and miserable principles? Do you wish to be enslaved by them all over again?" (Galatians 4:9).

6. Why is the world's standard of beauty "weak and miserable"?

7. What are some ways you can guard your heart to keep from becoming enslaved all over again by the world's definition of beauty?

8. Write a prayer in which you tell the Lord how much you love Him, repent for putting anything above your relationship with Him, and ask Him to place a new heart and a new understanding of His beauty within you.

For you know that it was not with perishable things such as silver or gold that you were redeemed from the empty way of life handed down to you from your forefathers, but with the precious blood of Christ, a lamb without blemish or defect.

—1 Peter 1:18-19

....4

A Modest Appeal

WE live in a world of skin. Everywhere we look, girls and women are revealing it. Bare midriffs, plunging necklines, and thigh-high skirts. The word *sexy* used to mean being ready and available for sex, but now it can mean anything from being fashionable to cute to beautiful. Sexy is in.

What comes to mind when you hear the word *modesty*? Floor-length skirts? Turtlenecks? Sack-like dresses? Contrary to what many think, modesty is not about hiding our bodies because they are shameful; it's about protecting them because they're valuable. When we dress modestly, we send the message that our bodies are not cheap.

No one takes a priceless gift and leaves it unguarded. We protect what we value. Our bodies are a priceless gift from God, and they deserve protection.

Putting on an outfit communicates more than our sense of

style; it communicates the condition of our heart. If our hearts are positioned toward the world, we'll dress to fit in. But if our hearts are positioned toward God, we will dress to please Him.

Our value is not determined by what we wear, but what we wear communicates what we *think* our value is. Pants that ride too low, shirts that show too much, or clothes that are too clingy send the message that we think our bodies are not worth protecting.

Most girls don't wake up in the morning thinking, "What can I wear today to entice somebody?" However, what we wear sends a message, and we're often unaware of what it is. We are so accustomed to immodesty, we seldom think about it. But we should. If we don't value our bodies by being modest, neither will others.

Have you ever had a day when you just felt . . . dumpy? Nothing looked right, your hair was crazy, and you had a huge zit on your face. These are "danger" days because a girl who feels bad about herself will try to raise her self-esteem by wearing small, tight-fitting clothes—even if she has to suck in her breath to get everything fastened. Wearing clothes that are too small can create a big modesty problem. If you can see the entire outline of your bra underneath your shirt, so can others. If your shirt clings to the outline of your breasts, or your jeans cling to the outline of your behind, others' eyes likely will cling to the same place.

Granted, seeing a woman's breasts is nothing new in our society. Actresses stroll the red carpet with dresses that plunge to their belly buttons, advertisements show women covering their naked breasts with their arms, and movies callously joke about the size of a woman's chest. But breasts—large or small—are a significant part of a woman's sexuality.

Advising a man to be faithful to his wife, Solomon said, "A loving doe, a graceful deer—may her breasts satisfy you always, may you ever be captivated by her love" (Proverbs 5:19). A woman's breasts were created to bring satisfaction to her husband. Not only do most men enjoy touching a woman's breasts, they enjoy seeing them—not because men are a bunch of perverts but because they were created to enjoy breasts. However, God's intention was that each man would see only one woman's breasts—his wife's.

Because we're desensitized to seeing breasts, most girls think it's no big deal if they wear a low-cut shirt. After all, they're not showing their whole chest, just the top. But whether it's the top, the middle, or the side, breasts are still breasts. For guys, seeing a "slice of the pie" is likely to make them think about the whole thing.

Low-cut tops aren't the only tricky area. If a neckline is too wide, breasts become visible when we bend over. Anyone standing nearby can see more than they should. Being short, I also have to make sure my shirts don't give someone taller an eyeful.

Dressing modestly requires creativity—and a lot of layering. With most shirts, it doesn't take much reaching or bending to expose your midriff. A camisole or t-shirt underneath can solve the problem.

Although we often limit a woman's sexuality to breasts and hips, other body parts also communicate sexuality.

You may not understand the power of a bared belly, but guys do. Consider the words of Solomon to his bride on their honeymoon night, "Your navel is a rounded goblet . . . Your waist is a mound of wheat encircled by lilies" (Song of Solomon 7:2).

You probably wonder what wheat and lilies have to do with being sexy. Beneath a woman's belly are her sexual organs and the place where conception takes place. For Solomon to express the beauty of his wife's belly was to express the beauty of her sexuality. He was married to her, so he had the right to see and enjoy this part of her body. However, when you bare your belly to just anyone, you diminish its value to your future husband.

Remember, modesty does not suggest that certain body parts are shameful but that our entire bodies are meant for one man's enjoyment—your future soul mate, your husband.

In her book *Secret Keeper: The Delicate Power of Modesty,* Dannah Gresh says, "God's purpose for you sexually is to 'intoxicate' one man. . . . When you dress immodestly, you create arousal in many men."[1]

When we value the powerful sexuality that God has given us, we choose to clothe our bodies with modesty. It means valuing our bodies enough to cover them.

Pants that are too tight are just as immodest as a skirt that is too short. You can be covered from head to toe in clothing and still be sensual. Remember, we want people to be drawn toward our hearts as they convey our love for God, not our bodies as they call attention to our flesh.

Because we are surrounded by sexual messages, we forget that our bodies are sexually powerful. Gresh explains:

> [The Gestalt theory] teaches a graphic designer to control a viewer's time by forcing the person to mentally complete a visual image. Because the brain is intrigued by completing the incomplete, it will always pause to finish an unfinished picture. . . . What does a guy see when a girl walks by him wearing a long, tight skirt with a slit all the way up the

sides? He sees past the fabric, [sic] because the slit invites him to finish the picture.[2]

Even if only ten percent of a skirt is immodest, the imagination will gravitate toward the ten percent. Keep it one hundred percent pure.

A few years ago, showing underwear was embarrassing. But times have changed, and underwear is now outerwear. From showing bra straps, to wearing lingerie as a shirt, to letting underwear ride above jeans, articles of clothing that once were meant to stay hidden have now become a part of the clothing ensemble.

When a girl dresses in a way that leaves an unfinished picture, she invites others to think about what they're not seeing. A bra strap leads to the bra, the underwear waistband to the underwear itself—and both lead a guy to think about the body parts they're covering. We can avoid these issues by making sure our underwear stays under what we wear—that's why it's called *under*wear.

Underwear with messages, some very suggestive, is another fad. Whenever we buy any clothing with messages on it (t-shirts or underwear), we need to ask ourselves if the message reflects what God thinks about us.

Clothes affect behavior. If you wear something cute, you feel cute; if you wear something comfortable, you feel relaxed. Likewise, if you wear something sexual (even though it may be underwear you don't intend anyone else to see), you feel sexual. When we feel sexual, we send off sexual signals. You may not even intend to act in a teasing way, but clothes that make you feel sexy will cause you to be more flirtatious than usual or to push past boundaries you don't intend to overstep.

One day as I was walking past the lingerie section of a local department store, I overheard the conversation of two young women. Stopping to look at thong and string bikini underwear on a display table, one girl said, "I can't wait to buy cute underwear like this." "Why would you need that?" her friend asked. "For when I get a boyfriend," the first girl responded.

My heart fell as I realized the thinking behind her words.

Some claim they wear thongs so no one can see the outline of their underwear through their pants. But if pants are tight enough to show the outline of underwear, they probably are tight enough to show the outline of a thong. What do you think is going to be more sexually stimulating for a guy—seeing the outline of a girl's bikini briefs or the outline of a thong?

One day when I was riding in a van one of the young girls a few seats ahead of me leaned forward to reach something on the floor. As she did, her pants rode down and her shirt rode up, leaving her bright red thong visible for all behind her to see. What really caught my attention were the bulging eyes of the guys sitting directly behind her.

Thongs are popular, but they are meant to be sexy and you are called to be virtuous. As girls, we just don't understand the strong connection between a guy's eyes and his sexual drive.

Great, you say, this discussion leaves me naked in the closet with nothing to wear. Not so. God does not expect us to do something that cannot be accomplished. If we're determined to walk in His beauty, He will give us the ability to be modest.

Here's a radical thought: what if you prayed before you shopped? God cares about the little details in your life as well as the big ones. Scripture tells us that God has the hairs on our heads numbered. If He cares enough to count hairs, He cares enough to help you shop. When God cares about something, He doesn't just tell us what to do, He enables us to do it. If He cares about modesty, He will provide the wisdom to make godly choices in what you wear.

That is—if you ask Him.

Remember, modesty is defined by your heart, and the things we treasure indicate the condition of our heart: "Where your treasure is, there your heart will be also" (Matthew 6:21).

Dressing immodestly indicates that you care more about fitting in with peers than reflecting the image of your Creator. You put your faith on display whenever you put your clothes on—or take them off.

The Israelites misused their God-given beauty in their worship of false gods. "At the head of every street you built your lofty shrines and degraded your beauty, offering your body with increasing promiscuity to anyone who passed by" (Ezekiel 16:25). Their bad choices brought harsh consequences. Because they did not understand or value their special relationship with God, they became slaves to other nations.

We too face a choice as to what we will do with the gift God has given us in our bodies. Too often we trade the precious beauty

God gives for the cheap, sexualized beauty the world offers. We end up trading something priceless for something that diminishes our value. When we try so hard to fit in with our culture, we don't realize what we've lost until it's gone.

That's what happened to the Israelites. They watched their city, their homes, and, most devastating of all, their temple be leveled to the ground by invading forces. One hundred and fifty years later they were still living in exile. Their sin had cost them their freedom, their identity, and their sense of belonging.

Later generations longed to return home after being given their freedom, but they had no home to return to. Their only option was to rebuild.

The temple had been the center of worship because God resided there. After rebuilding the temple, the Israelites discovered an important truth: They couldn't protect the temple without rebuilding the wall around the city. Restoring the temple would have done little good if they had left the city vulnerable to attack.

Finding our beauty in Christ is like restoring the temple, but the rebuilding doesn't end there. We still need a wall of protection. Being a young woman of true beauty requires the protective wall of modesty.

Building a wall of modesty is no easy task, but neither was rebuilding the wall of Jerusalem.

A man named Nehemiah was deeply grieved when he saw the wall of God's holy city in shambles. Nehemiah understood the importance of the wall, and he knew that the people would never truly be free without it.

"You see the trouble we are in," said Nehemiah. "Jerusalem

lies in ruins, and its gates have been burned with fire. Come, let us rebuild the wall of Jerusalem, and we will no longer be in disgrace" (Nehemiah 2:17).

A destroyed wall brings shame because an exposed city lacks strength and identity.

The world tells you that showing skin makes you beautiful, but it really just makes you naked and vulnerable.

Rebuilding the wall was costly for Nehemiah. When he arrived in Jerusalem, he rode around the city alone, surveyed the destruction, and considered the cost of restoration.

Obedience to the Lord is often costly and lonely. At times you may even be mocked for not looking like everyone else.

Just as Nehemiah and the people faced many challenges to rebuild the wall, you will face challenges in your efforts to rebuild the wall of modesty.

We have an enemy who "prowls around like a roaring lion looking for someone to devour" (1 Peter 5:8). Satan does not want you to understand God's design for beauty. One of the ways he controls you is by keeping you from seeing God's plan for beauty and thus keeping you from rebuilding the wall of modesty.

"Showing a little skin is no big deal," he will say. "If a guy lusts because of the way you dress, it's his problem, not yours," he will argue. "Modesty is old-fashioned," he will taunt. He may even suggest that modesty is a form of bondage to a list of rules.

But the enemy is a liar. As the story of Nehemiah shows, when we are faithful to do what God asks of us, God will make a way for the work to be completed.

The Israelites were able to rebuild the wall because they valued God's opinion more than man's (Nehemiah 6:16).

When you value God's opinion above all others, you will begin to see the true beauty of modesty.

Modesty does not require that you forsake fashion. It's possible to dress fashionably without compromising modesty. But if it did come down to a choice, which would you choose? Which do you value more: the approval of the world or of God? To whom are you more obedient—the world that doesn't know you or the God who created and formed you?

Discretion is not a word we usually associate with beauty, but it means "the ability to make responsible decisions, individual choice or judgment, the result of separating or distinguishing."[4]

A young woman who lacks discretion is unable to make a responsible decision. Desperate for the approval of others, she blindly follows fashion. Without discretion, her beauty is meaningless. Unprotected, beauty is used up and tossed out like trash. When we choose fashion over modesty, we are "a gold ring in a pig's snout," something precious wasted on something unclean.

There is no such thing as being just a little immodest. A little immodest is still immodest (Song of Solomon 2:15).

To become the woman God designed you to be, you must guard the wall of modesty that protects the temple of your body. Over time, little things like minor compromises can weaken your protection.

Our bodies were created to worship, not to be worshiped. We were made in God's image, and modesty indicates that we recognize our value and our need for protection.

Modesty isn't just about choosing what to wear—it's about knowing who we are: the temple of the living God.

Looking in the Mirror

1. In what ways has your view of modesty been shaped by the world?

2. Psalm 4:2-3a says, "How long, O men, will you turn my glory into shame? How long will you love delusions and seek false gods? Know that the LORD has set apart the godly for himself." How does our immodesty turn God's "glory into shame"?

3. What changes does God want you to make in how you think about modesty?

4. If you had to choose between being fashionable and being modest, which would you choose and why?

5. How does being a woman of modesty reflect love toward the guys around us?

6. Does what you wear reflect a desire to protect the guys around you?

7. How does 1 Corinthians 10:24 relate to the issue of modesty?

8. How can the choice to be modest impact the lives of other girls around you?

I counsel you to buy from me gold refined in the fire,

so you can become rich; and white clothes to wear,

so you can cover your shameful nakedness; and salve

to put on your eyes, so you can see.

—Revelation 3:18

.....5

THE BEAUTY OF FRIENDS

FRIENDS are a part of the beauty of life. Whether we're five years old and looking for someone to play with us or we're seventeen and looking for someone to go shopping, friends are important. But building good friendships isn't easy. The relationships that make life enjoyable can also make it difficult.

At times every girl feels as if she doesn't fit in. She may be the most popular girl at school or she may be seen as a misfit. No matter what her social status is, she knows how it feels to be left out. Having lots of friends does not mean that a girl feels free to be herself.

As a teenager, I thought I was the only girl who had ever hated herself. I assumed that other girls felt as beautiful as they looked to me. From what I could see, they didn't struggle with the same self-doubt that haunted me. Even though God gave me awesome friends in high school and in college, I didn't talk about my self-esteem issues because I didn't think they would understand.

I now see this as a strategy Satan uses to keep us from letting God heal our broken places. When we hide our true selves behind masks of protection, those same masks eventually make us feel trapped. We begin to believe that others would reject us if they knew the real person. Certain that we're alone in our struggle, we stay silent. And we stay broken.

Jennifer is afraid other girls will look down on her if she admits her insecurities. She's convinced they'll be unable to understand and will think she's crazy. Her lack of trust keeps her from sharing her heart.

Most girls are like Jennifer. They don't talk about matters of the heart and soul because they don't feel safe. Girls can be territorial and catty. They can also be ruthless in their cliques, gossip, and cruel comparisons.

But relationships don't have to be that way—and they shouldn't be.

After Jesus identified the greatest commandment, He stated the second greatest commandment: "Love your neighbor as yourself" (Matthew 22:39).

Loving others as ourselves isn't easy. The reason may have to do with how we feel about ourselves. How can you love others as yourself when you don't even like who you are?

Without meaning to, we use friends to measure our value. We want our friends to make us feel accepted and important. But friendships based on neediness are destined for hard times.

God gave us the desire to share our lives with others just as He gave us the desire for beauty. But we cannot find our beauty in friends; we can only express our beauty to and through them.

During my freshman year of college, my parents moved to

Georgia. I didn't care for the humidity, but I loved the impressive magnolia trees with their glossy leaves and big, cream-colored blossoms. When my parents bought a house in the country with an abundance of trees, my favorite was the magnolia tree in the front yard.

Even though I was supposed to be a "mature" college student, I loved to climb that tree. Sitting in the branches made me feel free. Final exams, relationships with guys, and fears about my future faded into the background as I swung myself up to sit in the cool shade of the strong, lower branches.

The beauty of that tree also taught me a valuable lesson. One of the traits of a magnolia tree is its large root system. Friendships are a lot like the thick branches and the beautiful blossoms of magnolia trees—they thrive because of a deep root system.

We want to have strong friendships and to enjoy the benefits of those relationships, but we can't do so unless the right kind of growth has taken place. If that tree had not had a strong root system, it would not have produced thick branches and beautiful blossoms. In the same way, if we are not rooted in the Lord, we will not grow strong branches that support friendships or beautiful blossoms that bring pleasure.

The more we understand how much He values us, the more we want God to be glorified in our thoughts, our actions, *and* our relationships. The awesome part of this is that the more we care about what God thinks, the more our relationships change to reflect the pure love Jesus talked about—

GOD'S WORD SAYS

[A]s the soil makes the sprout come up and a garden causes seeds to grow, so the Sovereign LORD will make righteousness and praise spring up before all nations. —Isaiah 61:11

"love your neighbor as yourself" (Matthew 22:39). When we become deeply rooted in Him, our lives naturally produce branches that reach out to others (Isaiah 61:11).

Righteousness grows out of a desire to serve the Lord despite what everyone else does. It grows in the midst of difficult struggles. And it grows when you surround yourself with people who fervently pursue the heart of God (Psalm 1:1-3).

GOD'S WORD SAYS

Blessed is the man who does not walk in the counsel of the wicked or stand in the way of sinners or sit in the seat of mockers. But his delight is in the law of the LORD, and on his law he meditates day and night. He is like a tree planted by streams of water, which yields its fruit in season and whose leaf does not wither. Whatever he does prospers.
—Psalm 1:1-3

A blessed young woman saturates herself in the Word because she cares more about what God values than what the world values.

Sometimes we underestimate the influence that others have over us. We think we are strong enough to be unaffected by the choices others make. However, the people we surround ourselves with indicate the direction our lives are going. Relationships either nourish or hinder our spiritual growth.

Always ready with a smile, Jordan is a fun-loving, walk-into-a-room-and-light-it-up kind of girl. While she's always been known as outgoing, Jordan is learning what it means to be a true friend and not just a "make everybody happy" person. God is teaching her to trust His opinion of her rather than the opinion of others. She is discovering her true beauty.

Jordan has also learned that finding her beauty in Christ involves making some difficult decisions. When a close friend was influencing her in a negative way, Jordan decided that her friend's approval wasn't worth compromising her convictions. Jordan chose to put some emotional distance in the friendship for a time. This didn't mean ignoring her friend—it simply meant not spending as much time together, not asking her friend for advice, and not getting caught up in her friend's negative behaviors.

By praying for her friend and being available to listen, Jordan is learning how to love her and yet still have safe boundaries. Because of Jordan's willingness to walk a difficult path, she has been able to maintain a relationship with her friend while modeling what it means to have a passionate relationship with the Lord.

When she was looking to her friend to find her value, Jordan couldn't see her own beauty in Christ. The result was an unhealthy friendship. But now, as she finds her beauty in Christ, Jordan is becoming the friend God designed her to be.

When you are wrapped up in loving God, you don't need to look to others for your value. Instead, you can do what God instructs us to do—to love others as you love yourself.

Friendships are good. Godly friendships are priceless. King David knew the importance of having trustworthy friends who were committed to the Lord. He made a commitment to surround himself with men who served God: "I am a friend to all who fear you, to all who follow your precepts" (Psalm 119:63).

Although peers influence the way we perceive ourselves, our closest friends have the greatest influence.

King David knew that the kind of people he spent the most time with would shape the kind of person he would be. He wanted friends who were committed to following God's teachings because he knew those friends would encourage him to pursue God's heart.

When it comes to the friends we *depend* on, the ones we are closest to, we need to follow King David's example by choosing friends who are committed to Christ—in their actions as well as in their words. It's one thing for a best friend to say she's a Christian; it's another for her to live as one.

To become the women God has created us to be, we need to surround ourselves with others who desire God's design for their lives above the desires of the world.

Are we called to reach out to those who don't have a relationship with Jesus? Absolutely. Christ Himself spent time with sinners. We are all called to reach out in love to those who do not know Christ. But Jesus didn't ask sinners for advice or lean on them in His time of need. In His greatest moment of anguish, He chose three of His disciples to accompany Him to pray.

GOD'S WORD SAYS

Don't become partners with those who reject God. How can you make a partnership out of right and wrong? That's not partnership; that's war. Is light best friends with dark?
—2 Corinthians 6:14 THE MESSAGE

To be intimate friends with someone is to know the deepest part of that person. If our relationship with Christ is at the deepest part of who we are, how can we be intimate friends with an unbeliever? (2 Corinthians 6:14).

As believers, we cannot have a deep, close, dependent relationship with someone who does not know Christ because our goals, values, and priorities are not the same. Jesus said, "He who is not with me is against me" (Matthew 12:30). To value Christ is to reject the world. To value the world is to reject Christ. You cannot have it both ways.

People who value the world want to talk, look, and act like the world. Is this what we want in our closest relationships? The people closest to us should be those we desire to be like, who desire to act like Christ, not the world.

As you think about your close friends, ask yourself: Are they more concerned about possessing the character of Christ or having the perfect figure? Are they more concerned about having a strong relationship with the Lord or getting a guy's attention? Are they more concerned about glorifying God with their bodies or with using their bodies to gain approval from the world?

If your close friends desire Christ more than the things of this world, consider yourself blessed and hang on to those friendships. If your answer is *I'm not sure*, talk with them about what they value in life. Knowing what your friends value is important because their values will become yours.

If you know your friends value the world more than they value Christ, search your heart to find out what draws you to them. If the friendships are pulling you away from your relationship with the Lord, distance yourself from those individuals. God can still use you to reach out to them, but you need safe boundaries. The friends with whom you are most vulnerable must be people who can give you godly advice and who desire to see you grow in the Lord.

If God is showing you that you need to separate from some of your friends, do so with love. Scripture tells us to speak the truth in love (Ephesians 4:15). Ask the

GOD'S WORD SAYS

[S]peaking the truth in love, we will in all things grow up into him who is the Head, that is, Christ. —Ephesians 4:15

Lord to give you the words you need to express truth in a loving way.

While it may be a lonely and difficult process to separate from close friends with whom you have been unequally yoked, God is faithful. He will be right beside you, and, in time, He will bring godly friends into your life. Just remember, it's hard to find a model friend if you're not willing to be one.

The beauty of Christ not only determines who our close friends are; it also changes the kind of friend we are.

When Megan's friend made a decision that hurt her, Megan wanted to walk away from the friendship. But she knew she couldn't. God had been showing her how much He loved her, and for the first time in her life Megan was seeing her beauty in Him. Rather than turning to gossip and backstabbing to get even, Megan chose to listen to her friend.

GOD'S WORD SAYS

The words of a gossip are like choice morsels; they go down to a man's inmost parts. —Proverbs 26:22

A perverse man stirs up dissension, and a gossip separates close friends. —Proverbs 16:28

Most girls would agree that gossip has the potential to destroy the person being talked about. But gossip does far more damage to the one telling the tale and the one listening than to the person being discussed (Proverbs 26:22).

Gossip becomes a part of us. While it might make us feel good for a moment, gossip eventually brings heartache (Proverbs 16:28).

Even godly girls can get caught up in the gossip game. But a girl who walks in His beauty "speaks the truth from [her] heart and has no slander on [her] tongue" (Psalm 15:2-3).

Megan and her friend realized that talking *about* each other wouldn't help the situation. The friendship could be restored only by talking *to* each other. They saw the connection between beauty and forgiveness. Because they chose to do things according to God's Word, they learned to love each other through some tough places. What could have been a true-to-life girl saga, with drama and rumors in abundance, instead became a real friendship.

Cliques, gossip, and wounded hearts don't have to be the norm. Rather than get jealous when your best friend brings a new girl along on your shopping trip, see it as an opportunity to show her Christ's love. Rather than be intimidated by girls who look as if they have it all together, take the time to get to know their stories and find out what's really going on in their lives. Rather than listen to trashy gossip about the popular girl so you can feel better about yourself, stand up for her and tell your friends you've been praying for her.

Let a beautiful heart make you a beautiful person.

Looking in the Mirror

1. What's the difference between being friendly to someone and being close friends with that person?

2. To discern whether or not your closest friends are godly role models, ask yourself the following questions about each of your intimate friends (remember our definition of intimate—someone with whom you share the deepest parts of who you are, someone with whom you spend a great deal of time).

■ Does she get excited when I talk about God?

■ Does she hold me accountable when I do something contrary to God's Word?

■ Does she respect me when I take a stand for my beliefs?

3. To discern whether or not you need to separate from a friend who may be pulling you away from the Lord, ask yourself the following questions about each of your friends.

■ Do I argue more with my parents and others in authority when I hang around her?

■ Does she do things that contradict God's Word?

■ Do I do things that contradict God's Word when I'm with her?

■ Do I have a harder time hearing and obeying God when I'm with her?

4. Would you consider yourself to be a model friend? Why or why not?

5. How does the way you feel about your beauty affect your friendships?

6. Have you ever been jealous of another girl? Why? How did that jealousy affect your relationship with her? How did it affect how you felt about yourself?

7. Write a prayer asking God to teach you how to be a model friend and to give you friends who desire to serve Him.

The righteous should choose . . . friends carefully,

for the way of the wicked leads them astray.

−Proverbs 12:26 NKJV

......6

Model Mentors

KINSEY had trouble getting her family to understand her interest in spiritual things. Her mom and dad went to church on Sunday, but they didn't get involved beyond that. Their Bibles remained untouched during the week. Family prayer consisted of the blessing said before dinner each night. When Kinsey wanted to talk about the Lord and what she was learning, her parents didn't seem to know how to respond.

They would look at her, furrow their brows, and tell her she should spend less time reading her Bible and more time getting involved in school activities to build her college resumé. Kinsey figured that deep down they were afraid she would end up being some religious fanatic, perhaps even working in foreign missions.

But Kinsey knew a woman who listened and understood. Sarah studied the Word, prayed for those around her, and encouraged Kinsey in her relationship with the Lord. Always quick to admit that she was far from perfect, Sarah shared with Kinsey what she had learned through her own struggles with the Lord. She admitted that her faith was still being stretched, and Kinsey loved her genuineness. Like Sarah, Kinsey wanted God to change every part of her to honor Him.

Sarah always made it clear to Kinsey that her parents needed to know what was going on in her life whether or not they understood. "The Lord speaks to people's hearts far beyond what we see," Sarah would say.

Some of the other girls at church didn't understand why Kinsey talked to Sarah. They saw Sarah's graying hair, her *Southern Living* magazines, and her Cadillac DeVille and assumed she couldn't possibly relate. They preferred going to their friends for advice. Kinsey, however, had grown up watching Sarah's life, and she saw something in Sarah that she wanted. Kinsey didn't know what to call it, but she knew it was good.

What Kinsey saw in Sarah was the beauty of age, the beauty of wisdom. Whenever Kinsey had a difficult decision to make, she knew where to go. This time was no different.

Answering Kinsey's light knock, Sarah opened the door and welcomed her with her usual gentle smile. "It's good to see you, Kinsey. Is everything okay? You've been on my heart today, and I've been praying for you."

Sarah continued talking as she led Kinsey toward the kitchen where a pot of Tiramisu-flavored coffee was brewing. Peace settled over Kinsey as she sat comfortably at Sarah's kitchen table and began to open her heart. Kinsey knew she had come to the right place.

The right perspective is essential. Everything we see shapes our understanding. Much of the time our vision is limited to whatever is in front of us. Focused on our own struggles, we don't see that others have faced the same self-esteem issues. Discovering our beauty is a difficult and treacherous journey. We need someone who understands what we're going through—someone who has walked through difficult places ahead of us.

Prior to my freshman year in college, I went on a hiking trip to the Adirondack Mountains. My previous camping experiences had been mainly at campgrounds with swimming pools, so I was unprepared for this trip. The all-day hikes were challenging enough, but I hit a wall on the day we had to bushwhack up the side of a mountain. No longer were we following a trail. A compass was our only marker. The journey seemed endless as we worked our way over fallen logs and through tightly knit pine trees. I wanted to sit down and cry.

My perspective was limited to what I could see in front of me—trees, trees, and more trees. The guides, however, had made the journey before, so their perspective was much different from mine. They knew that the view awaiting us was extraordinary.

During the hike, I secretly wished they would call in a helicopter to airlift me to the top of the mountain so my struggle would be over. But when we reached the top of the mountain, I understood why our guides had persisted in pushing us onward. The overwhelming sense of awe and accomplishment I felt when I arrived at the top was unforgettable.

The challenge to understand our true value and worth is like hiking to the top of those mountains. Some days you doubt whether you can make it past all the barriers—deceitful advertisements, godless influences, and seductive messages—that stand in your way.

Women who are wiser and more experienced can help you see beyond your circumstances. Godly women know that finding true beauty requires pushing past the barriers that block your way. Pressing you on toward the heart of God, they challenge you to keep your focus on His beauty. As they share their testimonies of God's faithfulness, you learn that finding your true worth is possible.

When I think about the value of having an older, wiser woman as a role model, the relationship between Elizabeth and Mary in the New Testament comes to mind. Although their experiences differed greatly, God brought them to a similar place. They shared the most important quality two women can share—a desire to serve the Lord.

Elizabeth was "upright in the sight of God, observing all the Lord's commandments and regulations blamelessly" (Luke 1:6). Mary, according to the angel Gabriel, was "highly favored" (1:28). One older and wiser, one young and uncertain, each carried within her womb a promise from God.

As an unmarried, pregnant young woman, Mary had few people she could go to for advice and support. After hearing the angel's news, she turned to Elizabeth, a godly woman she could confide in and trust. Conceiving a child through the Holy Spirit is not your average teenage crisis! No wonder Mary got ready and hurried to Elizabeth's home (1:39).

As soon as Mary stepped into her house, Elizabeth began to talk about God's promises for Mary. Mary had not even had time to tell Elizabeth about her visit from the angel. The Holy Spirit had revealed Mary's condition to Elizabeth, so she was able to speak confidently about the situation.

Elizabeth also spoke encouragement to Mary. Mary didn't understand what was happening, and Elizabeth encouraged her to believe that God would do what He promised. She said to Mary, "Blessed is she who has believed that what the Lord has said to her will be accomplished" (1:45). Elizabeth didn't answer all of Mary's questions or resolve all of her concerns. She simply encouraged Mary to believe and trust the Lord.

Girls sometimes write off the advice of older women because they think that an older woman couldn't possibly understand their world or relate to their situations.

Elizabeth didn't have to wear hip clothes, listen to popular music, or know the latest slang to have an impact on Mary's life. Mary saw Elizabeth's godly character and knew that Elizabeth had much guidance to offer.

Elizabeth had something to offer Mary that Mary's friends did not have. Elizabeth provided perspective. When we're in the middle of difficult or confusing times, we need someone outside of the situation who can help us see clearly. Our vision is limited by things in the here and now. Older women can help us see down the road.

Godly women offer not only love and encouragement but wisdom as well. A model mentor knows how to apply what she has learned from the Word to her life. You may not always like what she has to say, but you need to hear the truth she speaks to you in love (Ephesians 4:15). Because she's committed to seeing you grow in the Lord, she's willing to point out areas where you're compromising your God-given beauty. More importantly, she's willing to stick by you as you learn to see your true beauty.

While it would be nice to be able to walk into a store and pick out a model mentor, life doesn't happen that way. Finding a mentor is a process, and it requires both choosing and being chosen. But it doesn't have to be complicated. Simply watch the lives of women around you, ask the Lord for direction, and be willing to invest in the relationship.

In the ancient world, a young Moabite woman named Ruth learned to serve the Lord by watching her mother-in-law, Naomi. After the death of her husband, Ruth made a covenant to stay with Naomi even though Naomi had decided to return to her homeland.

The world idolizes people, but it focuses on how a person looks rather than who she is. Caught in the trap of physical perfection, we try to shape our life after the model on the cover of the magazine. We read about her diet and exercise program. We follow the magazine's tips for perfect hair and makeup, and we imitate the fashion styles we see these beautiful women wearing. But imitating the life of a physically perfect woman does not point us to anything beyond herself. Our value becomes limited to how well we mimic the look rather than bringing us to a deeper understanding of God's character and love.

"Don't urge me to leave you or to turn back from you," Ruth urged Naomi. "Where you go I will go, and where you stay I will stay. Your people will be my people and your God my God. Where you die I will die, and there I will be buried. May the LORD deal with me, be it ever so severely, if anything but death separates you and me" (Ruth 1:16-17).

Why would anyone leave home, culture, and family—essentially everything familiar—to go to a place where life would be completely different? For that very reason—life would be completely different. Ruth had been raised in Moab, among people who worshiped many gods. Naomi was an Israelite who worshiped one God. Ruth saw something in Naomi's life that she wanted. Ruth saw the One, true God. Something in Naomi's life made Ruth desire Naomi's God.

When we think about finding a model mentor we need to look for someone who worships the one true God, not wealth, education, possessions, positions, or appearances.

Imitating the life of a godly woman drives us to search deeper to know the heart of God.

When we ask the Lord for direction, He will show us women we can learn from. Model mentors come in all shapes and sizes. There is no one-size-fits-all. But there are some general characteristics to look for. A model mentor should be . . .

- Passionate about the Lord (Psalm 84:2).
- A doer of the Word and not just a hearer (James 1:23-25).
- Fully engaged in life but unaffected by the world (1 Peter 2:11-12).

GOD'S WORD SAYS

My soul yearns, even faints, for the courts of the Lord; my heart and my flesh cry out for the living God. —Psalm 84:2

Anyone who listens to the word but does not do what it says is like a man who looks at his face in a mirror and, after looking at himself, goes away and immediately forgets what he looks like. But the man who looks intently into the perfect law that gives freedom, and continues to do this, not forgetting what he has heard, but doing it—he will be blessed in what he does. —James 1:23-25

Dear friends, I urge you, as aliens and strangers in the world, to abstain from sinful desires, which war against your soul. Live such good lives among the pagans that, though they accuse you of doing wrong, they may see your good deeds and glorify God on the day he visits us. —1 Peter 2:11-12

Not that I have already obtained all this, or have already been made perfect, but I press on to take hold of that for which Christ Jesus took hold of me. Brothers, I do not consider myself yet to have taken hold of it. But one thing I do: Forgetting what is behind and straining toward what is ahead, I press on toward the goal to win the prize for which God has called me heavenward in Christ Jesus.

All of us who are mature should take such a view of things. And if on some point you think differently, that too God will make clear to you. —Philippians 3:12-15

The watchman opens the gate for him, and the sheep listen to his voice. He calls his own sheep by name and leads them out. When he has brought out all his own, he goes on ahead of them, and his sheep follow him because they know his voice. But they will never follow a stranger; in fact, they will run away from him because they do not recognize a stranger's voice. —John 10:3-5

- Willing to admit she's still learning (Philippians 3:12-15).
- Able to discern the voice of the Lord (John 10:3-5).

She also should have beauty radiating from within.

God brought Naomi and Ruth together, but it was Ruth's decision to pursue a relationship.

We develop relationships most naturally with those we see often. Ruth could not have had a relationship with Naomi if she had remained in Moab, so she chose to go where Naomi was going. True mentorship develops out of a relationship. True mentorship takes place when you spend time with the woman God brings across your path. Share your heart with her, and listen to what she has learned in her relationship with the Lord.

If you ask Him, God will bring godly women into your life. But you must be willing to pursue a relationship. You must let these women into your life, hear their advice, and follow it when it lines up with God's Word.

Ruth saw the value in Naomi's counsel. She trusted Naomi because Naomi trusted the Lord. Ruth's obedience and her willingness to trust Naomi's advice brought Ruth and her future husband, Boaz, together.

In the end, both Ruth and Naomi experienced great blessing from their relationship. Ruth discovered great wisdom; Naomi found comfort in her sadness; and both women learned that life was full of beauty. When Ruth gave birth to Naomi's first grandson, the women around Naomi told her, "'Praise be to the Lord, who this day has not left you without a kinsman-redeemer. May he become famous throughout Israel! He will renew your life and sustain you in your old age. For your daughter-in law, who loves you and who is better to you than seven sons, has given him birth" (Ruth 4:14-15).

As with Ruth and Naomi, a model relationship must be based upon faith in the Lord and obedience to the Word. God has created us to be unique individuals; we are not to become a clone of someone else. However, in the same way that Paul encouraged early believers to follow his example as he followed the example of Christ, we look to godly women because they teach us how to look like Christ (1 Corinthians 11:1). When God brings a model mentor into your life, He does not expect you to become exactly like her. You are to watch how she applies God's truth to her decisions, follow her example, and learn to put the Word into practice in your own life.

> ## GOD'S WORD SAYS
>
> Follow my example, as I follow the example of Christ. —1 Corinthians 11:1

God doesn't expect us to become beautiful on our own. He gives us living examples of His beauty in the women He brings into our lives. Able to see much farther down the road than we can, these godly women walk the journey with us if we train our eyes to see their value. Opening our hearts to hear their stories, we share our lives with them and trust the beauty we see in them.

Looking in the Mirror

1. What's the difference between someone speaking into your life and someone trying to control your life?

2. Identify a time when God has used a more experienced woman to speak into your life. What did you learn through this experience?

3. What kinds of things does an older woman have to offer you that you can't find in relationships with girls your own age?

4. Who are some godly women in your life? What makes them beautiful according to God's standard?

5. Read 1 Corinthians 11:1. What can you learn from this Scripture about finding a mentor? What kinds of things should you look for in that woman's life?

6. Read Psalm 101:6. What does it mean for someone to have a "walk [that is] blameless"? Why does David allow only those who are faithful to minister to him?

7. Why is it important to choose carefully the people we allow to guide us?

Young people take pride in their strength, but the
gray hairs of wisdom are even more beautiful.
–Proverbs 20:29 Contemporary English Version

.......7

LIKE MOTHER, LIKE DAUGHTER

IRLS are made for relationship. Not many guys stress out over their friendships or spend hours analyzing their interactions. Girls, however, can spend days rethinking one conversation. So why do we care so much? Because the way we feel about ourselves determines how we interact with others. In the same way, how others respond to us determines how we feel about ourselves. And since people often respond to us on the basis of how we look, beauty and relationships get all wrapped up in unhealthy ways.

Since relationships begin at home, so does our understanding of beauty. Before girls begin reading fashion magazines or swapping clothes with best friends, they learn from their moms. Moms show daughters how to apply makeup, coordinate an outfit, and sit in a skirt. Through their relationship, moms teach daughters about beauty.

When God made moms, He gave them the ability to nurture. In this, they reflect His nurturing heart. Describing his relationship with the Lord, David wrote, "But I have learned to feel safe and satisfied, just like a young child on its mother's lap" (Psalm 131:2 CONTEMPORARY ENGLISH VERSION). God designed moms to be a safe place for children. Moms provide support, comfort, and belonging.

Relationships can be complicated, though, especially between a mom and a daughter. Some moms and daughters are alike while others couldn't be more different. Girls relate based on what they see and hear and how they feel. So a girl learns about beauty by seeing how her mom acts, hearing what her mom says, and responding to how her mom makes her feel.

What I See

Two peas in a pod. That's how most people describe Kelly and her mom. Both go-getters, they seem most content when they're busy. Not wanting to waste a moment, Kelly knows how to accomplish several things at once. She and her mom are organized, dependable, and masters of making the impossible happen.

Not only do they seem to do everything with ease, but they always look great doing it. Whether she's going to the mall with friends, heading to school, or out running, Kelly doesn't let down her guard. Like her mom, she has an outfit for every occasion and a beauty routine performed with precision.

She doesn't stop to think about why she lives this way; it's all she's ever known. Because of her dad's job, Kelly's family is well known. Kelly and her mom work hard to be what others expect the women in her father's life to be. Instead of drawing them closer, however, the pressure makes Kelly feel restless around her mom.

When they're together, Kelly is constantly trying to figure out what her mom thinks about her. They never just sit and talk. Kelly wants her mom to see past the way she looks. She wants her mom to see her for who she is and not just for what she does. Unable to see her mom's heart, Kelly sees only her desire to have it all together and assumes the same is expected of her.

Moms know they're being watched. But sometimes they forget which eyes are most important. It's easy for a mom to get caught up worrying about what other people think and completely forget about what life lessons she is teaching her daughter in the process.

Like her mom, Kelly plays the game of looking good on the outside while feeling broken on the inside. Beauty becomes something she puts on to please others.

She asks, *Will I ever measure up?*

What I Hear

Lindsey and her mom have very different personalities. Lindsey's temperament is more like her dad's. Her older sister, however, is like her mom, so the two of them have a great relationship, which makes Lindsey feel left out. Her relationship with her mom has always been difficult, but the older Lindsey gets the more difficult it becomes.

Shopping trips are torture for Lindsey. Her mom and sister always head toward the same racks. Lindsey wrinkles her nose with disdain every time they say, "Oh that's so cute." After her mother pays for the purchases, Lindsey reluctantly carries the bags of clothes. To her, they represent who her mom wants her to be. *Will the feeling of being alone ever end?* she wonders. She spends her days wishing she could just be herself and her nights crying herself to sleep.

To relieve her anger, Lindsey often resorts to sarcasm. Instead of helping the situation, Lindsey's words only hurt her mom. Thinking that Lindsey is just insecure, her mom tries to help by encouraging her to let her sister do her makeup. Her sister, the beauty queen. Being compared to her sister makes Lindsey feel as if God forgot her when He distributed beauty genes. Her mom's suggestion makes Lindsey feel even more awkward and unsure of herself. When she finally gives in and allows her sister to do her makeup, she feels like a clown.

Being a teenager isn't easy, but neither is being the mom of a teenager. Without meaning to, a mom can send her daughter hurtful messages about beauty. "Straighten your shirt." "You aren't really going out looking like that, are you?" "Why don't you try something different with your hair?"

Seemingly harmless suggestions still hurt.

In the game of comparison someone always gets hurt, especially if a girl is being measured against her own sister. Words of comparison, even those spoken in an attempt to help, leave a girl believing that beauty means becoming someone other than who she is.

She asks, *Why is who I am never good enough?*

What I Feel

Amanda shuts off her music after finishing her homework. She's had trouble concentrating and is relieved to have it done. She needs to talk, so she heads toward the family room, walking quietly to avoid waking up her siblings.

Amanda's mom is focused on her computer screen. The papers spread around her tell the tale of another late night trying to meet a deadline for her job. Amanda wants to spend time with her mom, but she doesn't want to add to her mom's already packed schedule. Whether she's driving Amanda's younger siblings to all their activities, tackling household chores, or finishing work left over from the day, Amanda's mom always has something more important than Amanda.

When she asks her mom if they can talk, her mom says, "Sure." But she continues to work on whatever is in front of her. Amanda senses her distraction. She knows her mom wants to get back to the task at hand. She believes that her mom loves her, but she can't help feeling as if she's an unwelcome interruption.

Amanda's mom is much more comfortable talking about what Amanda is doing than what she's feeling. Amanda gets involved in lots of school activities because it's the one thing she and her mom can talk about. Amanda wants to share her life with her mom, but even more she wants to share her heart. If only her mom would really listen.

Moms are busy. But a mom who's too busy to listen makes her daughter feel unimportant. Feelings are important, and so is a girl's need to be able to talk to her mom. No one wants to feel like an item on her mom's "to do" list.

Feeling left out of her mom's life, Amanda relates in the only way she knows how. She tries to meet her need to feel beautiful in the way she's been taught: by staying busy. But she is still uncertain of her worth and uncertain of her beauty. Like her relationship with her mom, beauty is something distant and disconnected from her life.

She asks, *Will I ever have any value?*

Struggling to Relate

No relationship is perfect, and some level of conflict between moms and daughters is normal. A butterfly must struggle to break free from its cocoon in order to strengthen its wings before taking flight. Without struggle, there is no independence. The same is true in mother-daughter relationships. The struggles bring maturity. They enable you to form your own individuality. They teach you to deal with conflict. They reveal areas where you still need to grow. The problem comes when there's so much conflict that the two of you have no relationship.

Maybe you can't even imagine a healthy relationship with your mom. Perhaps you turn away when you see girls shopping or having lunch with their moms because your relationship with your mom brings only pain. Hearing constant words of criticism, you feel as if you'll never measure up.

Maybe your mom moves from relationship to relationship trying to find her own value. If so, she probably detaches from you to become attached to a man, making you feel unimportant. Her search for love leaves you wondering where you fit in. Maybe she won't allow you into her world and she shows no interest in getting into yours. She can't relate to you, and seemingly doesn't even try.

God, however, did not create moms and daughters to make one another miserable. Something that is broken does not accomplish the purpose for which it was designed. A broken relationship with your mom will not work the way God designed it. But God wants to heal every part of your life, including your relationship with your mom.

God sent Jesus to "bind up" the brokenhearted (Isaiah 61:1). The phrase *bind up* means "to wrap firmly." When we give our lives to Jesus, He heals our hearts.

Understanding Her Story

Caught up in our own self-esteem issues, we find it hard to step back and see our moms as real women with real opinions and real struggles. Instead, we expect them to know what we need, understand what we think, and be able to relate to what's going on in our lives. All without interfering in our personal space.

True relationship, though, like true beauty, requires that we see beyond our own story to God's design. Regardless of where you are in your relationship with your mom, God wants you to see this relationship through His eyes. He wants you to see your mom as He sees her. You might think this task is impossible, especially if you and your mom have difficulty finishing a conversation without arguing. But it can be done.

Learning to understand your mom begins by learning to listen. Like you, she has a story. Like you, she has been wounded. And like you, she longs to know she's beautiful.

My mom is naturally beautiful, but for a long time she couldn't see her own beauty. She was more comfortable defining her value based on her intelligence. She considered beauty, as the world sees it, simply beyond her reach.

Beauty took too much time. Occasionally she would buy new makeup, but within a few weeks the products were pushed to the back of her bathroom drawer. Beauty wasn't worth the time.

Beauty also meant effort and frustration. At four feet, eleven inches, my mom was far from matching the image of long-legged females that the world valued. Finding stylish clothes was difficult, and finances ultimately determined her choices.

Unable to see her God-given beauty, she put her energy into finding her value in other areas. But ignoring her beauty didn't make her questions go away.

Listening to my mom share stories from her life, I have learned how her ideas about beauty were shaped by her experiences.

As the oldest of eight children, she had to be practical. She was responsible for taking care of her younger siblings and helping out around the house. When it came time for her to buy clothes for college, she didn't even know how to shop for herself. Her mom had never been able to teach her. Not enough time and not enough money left my mom on her own when it came to answering questions about beauty.

She also watched her own mother struggle to know her worth. My grandparents had significant problems in their marriage. From watching her own mother, my mom learned that all the makeup, jewelry, and coordinating shoes in the world couldn't convince a woman of her value. My grandmother used beauty as a mask to keep others from knowing how much she hurt inside. So when it came time for my mother to teach my sister and me about beauty, she felt inadequate.

The more I listen to my mom's story, the more I understand the gift she has given me in teaching me what she has. She certainly has given me more than she received. From my mom, I've learned that . . .

Beauty means strength.

Beauty means forgiveness.

Beauty means honesty.

Listen to more than just what your mom says. Learn to hear the message coming from her heart. Learn to understand her story.

Seeing Her Beauty

We assume that our moms have all of their beauty questions answered, but their wounds from the past affect their understanding of beauty, and so do the voices they hear as adults. Moms hear the same messages you do. But for moms, who are aging, the voices are even harsher because beauty is equated with looking young.

Whether your mom spends hours in front of the mirror or no time at all, take the time to consider what your mother thinks about herself. Just as you were designed for beauty, so is she.

Your mom doesn't have to fit some formula to be beautiful, and neither do you. True beauty comes from understanding your value in Christ. In the same way, understanding your mom's true beauty comes only when you see her through His eyes.

Can you see your mom's beauty? Does she know she's beautiful?

Looking in the Mirror

1. What have you learned about beauty through your relationship with your mom?

2. Do you see your mom as beautiful? Why or why not?

3. Read Psalm 119:169. How can the Lord help you to understand your mom's story? How can this understanding change your relationship with her?

4. How has your mom's story affected her understanding of beauty?

5. List five things you appreciate about your mom.

6. Sometimes loving your mom can be a struggle, especially if you've been hurt by her. Read Romans 5:5. What does it teach us about how we can love our moms even when it is difficult?

7. Think about the way you talk to your mom. Do your words show her you see her as a beautiful woman? Read Ephesians 4:29. How does this Scripture apply to your relationship with your mom?

8. How can understanding your own beauty change your relationship with your mom?

For the LORD gives wisdom, and from his mouth come

knowledge and understanding.

–Proverbs 2:6

8

HER DAD'S EYES

ONE of my favorite childhood memories is snuggling under the covers of my bed on stormy nights. As I listened to the rain against my bedroom window, I could hear the sounds of my father composing at the piano in the room below. I knew that he was sitting under the soft glow of the piano light with his favorite pencil in his mouth, his hands moving across the keyboard. Play, pause, erase, scribble, play. The rhythm of his music played against the rhythm of the rain.

I felt safe. I felt loved.

My dad was not a perfect father. Part of my struggle to love myself came from watching my dad face the same struggles. But one thing my dad did right was to give me the assurance that he loved me. I knew my dad cared about me and would do anything to protect me. Most of all, I knew that I belonged to him.

The relationship between fathers and daughters is incredibly powerful. Dads teach daughters how a girl should expect others to treat her, especially guys. Dads teach daughters that they're worth protecting, worth fighting for, and that they're beautiful.

God designed dads to cherish their daughters, but that is seldom conveyed in popular media. In television and movies dads are portrayed as detached and generally clueless as to how to relate to women, including their daughters. Busy with careers, new relationships, or their own interests, dads arrive on the scene only in a time of crisis, apparently unaware of how much their daughters need their time and attention.

Some girls have never known their dads; others have watched their fathers walk out at a significant time in their lives; still others see their dads spend endless hours on the job, on the golf course, or even at church. Being fatherless is more than just not having a dad. To be fatherless is to miss out on the relationship God intended between a dad and his daughter.

Talk

Girls thrive on words. Most of us can talk forever about a single little incident. We talk when we're mad. We talk when we're happy. We talk when we're scared. We talk when we're excited. And even if we aren't talking, our minds are still reeling with words.

Because words are so much a part of who we are, the words we hear shape our self-esteem. A dad gives his daughter direction and strength through his words. When our dads cheer for us, we feel the freedom to try new things. Dad's encouraging words give us the stamina to keep pressing on even when we make a mistake.

However, if a girl hears only negative words, or even silence, from her father, she feels like a failure. Overwhelmed by criticism, she tries even harder to gain her dad's approval. But no matter what she achieves, she believes she is a disappointment if she receives no affirmation from him.

Jamie is one of the most organized people you could ever meet. Her clothes hang neatly in her closet, her desk is organized, and her bed is made every morning. Jamie defines neatness. Whether at school or at home, she works hard at everything. Always the first to finish class projects, she's on top of things weeks before they happen. Her friends look at her in amazement, wondering if there's anything she can't do. She's the queen of control.

Underneath her orderly life, however, Jamie feels worthless. Nothing she does seems to please her father. Rather than hearing words of love and appreciation, the words Jamie hears are critical and angry. Or worse, her dad gives her the silent treatment to let her know he is unhappy with her.

She knows he's not really angry at her. He's angry at life. She could never be perfect enough to erase the hurts he has experienced. But knowing the reason doesn't fill the void in her heart. Only forgiveness brings healing.

Girls who receive no positive words often move into unhealthy relationships because they're looking for someone to tell them they have value. Unable to handle the silence of being alone, they go from one boyfriend to the next seeking approval and affirmation. They may even become sexually active because they think they have to trade sex for positive words. They simply want to know their lives have value. All girls look for someone who cares enough to speak words of protection and value to them.

My dad was never a big talker. Surrounded by all women

(except the dog), my dad listened at least three times as much as he talked. When he did talk, he put a lot of thought into his words. Unless of course I had pushed every last one of his buttons, and then the proverbial "think before you speak" went out the window. For the most part, though, my dad was careful with his words.

One day my dad looked at me and said, "He's not good enough for you." I was in high school and I was head over heels for one of the guys at our church. I thought I had hidden my feelings pretty well, but apparently I hadn't.

I was crushed that my dad didn't like the guy I thought I was in love with. Later, though, I came to see that it wasn't so much that my father thought badly about the guy; my dad thought highly of me. He thought I was something precious and worth protecting. He could see the qualities in me and the plans God had for me, and he knew this guy and I were not headed in the same direction.

When a dad takes the time to talk to his daughter and tell her the potential he sees in her, he shows his daughter that her thoughts and ideas are worth listening to. He shows his daughter she's worth his words.

Time

A dad may be present in body but absent from life. When he comes home at night, he walks past her room. But when he looks in and sees her busy watching television or doing her homework, he doesn't stop to talk. He thinks she doesn't need him. Sadly, she doesn't know how to tell him she does. Her IM buddies know more about her life than her dad does. Simply seeing her dad across the dinner table isn't enough to satisfy a daughter's desire to know that she's worth loving.

When someone wants to spend time with us, we feel valued and accepted. On the flip side, when someone doesn't spend time with us we feel rejected. A daughter whose dad isn't around assumes that something is wrong with her. There might be countless reasons for her dad's absence, but a girl can't see them. All she sees is his lack of time for her and thus concludes that she's not as important as everything else in his life.

Sarah's friends think she's strong, but sometimes she's too strong. To keep from getting hurt, she keeps people at a distance, even her best friends. She tells them only bits and pieces of her story. Because she doesn't feel safe, she doesn't trust anyone. But eventually the walls she built to protect herself make her feel trapped.

Sarah's parents have always been good providers, and she knows they care about her. But they have their world and she has hers. Her dad tells her he loves her, but when it comes to handling "stuff," Sarah is on her own. Not wanting to inconvenience anyone, she has developed her own coping devices to survive.

Girls need the safety of their fathers' love. Dads can't keep their daughters safe if they aren't aware of what's going on. A dad's words are incredibly important, but if they are not backed up by time and attention they lose their impact. Girls need dads who say, "I love you," and then prove it by making them a priority.

Sarah doesn't blame her dad for the bad decisions she made, but she now knows that she wasn't equippped to handle life on her own. She was designed to need her dad.

Touch

When his daughter starts growing up, a dad has to rethink the way he relates to her. No longer wanting to play with dolls and dress up, his daughter starts talking about bras, PMS, and boys. Gone is the little girl he used to swing into the air. In her place is a girl becoming a woman. He sees her body changing and becomes unsure about how to respond. Rather than enter the unknown world of womanhood, he backs away and lets mom handle the girl stuff.

To a daughter who's going through a lot of change, especially in her body, this pulling away is confusing. She used to snuggle in his lap as he read the newspaper. But now she feels unwelcome. So she too pulls away, and the gap in their relationship widens.

But sometimes it's not the *lack* of touch that damages a girl's relationship with her dad.

My friend Anna is one of the most precious women I know. She isn't afraid to walk through the valleys of life with me, and she isn't afraid to see the real me. She's a get-on-your-knees woman of God, and her faith makes her truly beautiful. But realizing her beauty has been a hard-fought battle for Anna.

Early in life Anna learned to use her appearance to cover her feelings. Although her parents considered themselves Christians, they were more concerned about looking good than being good. Anna tried to hide her inner pain by following their example, but still she hoped that someone would see through the hide-and-seek game she was playing. After all, how do you walk up to someone and say that your relationship with your dad isn't like that of other girls? How do you make people understand why you want to run away from the very man who should be protecting you? And how do you explain that you want your father to love you, just not in "that way"?

So Anna did what a lot of girls do when their experience of love and sexuality come together in a way that God never intended. Wanting to know that she was worth loving, and thinking that sex was the price she had to pay to feel loved, she gave away more than she should have to the guys she dated. But this search for value cost Anna her self-worth.

Sexual abuse is not something we talk about openly in the church. We assume it happens only among families outside our communities of faith. Sadly, that is not the case. Dads who talk to or touch their daughters in a sexual manner are violating God's design for dads.

Girls are made to be held and loved. A dad should teach his daughter that her body belongs to God. When he protects and respects her, he teaches her that her body should not be used by others. Through the way he hugs and holds his daughter, a dad teaches her appropriate boundaries for how others should treat her.

A dad provides for his daughter because she needs nourishment to grow into the woman God intends her to be. A dad gives his daughter a sense of identity and belonging because his daughter is a part of him. A dad protects his daughter because she is worth fighting for. A dad teaches his daughter that she's valuable, that she's beautiful, because that's what God intended.

The Father's Eyes

God is the ultimate Father. Whatever your relationship with your dad is like, God cares for you as a Father. He wants you to know you're worth protecting. He wants you to feel secure in His love. And He wants you to know you are priceless.

A good relationship with our dads allows us to glimpse God's heart. He has time to listen to what's going on in our lives. He watches over us to keep us from getting hurt. He wraps his arms around us when we're having a bad day. A dad who reflects God's heart makes his daughter feel loved.

But not all dads reflect God's heart. A girl who has been hurt by her dad has a hard time seeing how perfect God's love is. The hurts make it harder for her to trust God's love for her. She looks at her relationship with her dad and expects God to treat her the same way.

If your dad doesn't have time for you, you may see God as distant. If your dad constantly criticizes you, you may see God as always disappointed or even angry with you. If your dad makes promises and never keeps them, you may see God as undependable.

But God is none of these. He is a God of His word. When He says He will always love you, He means it (Numbers 23:19; Romans 8:38-39).

He says,

GOD'S WORD SAYS

God is not a man, that he should lie, nor a son of man, that he should change his mind. Does he speak and then not act? Does he promise and not fulfill? —Numbers 23:19

For I am convinced that neither death nor life, neither angels nor demons, neither the present nor the future, nor any powers, neither height nor depth, nor anything else in all creation, will be able to separate us from the love of God that is in Christ Jesus our Lord. —Romans 8:38-39

Before the beginning of time, I knew you. I knew what color your eyes would be, and I could hear the sound of your laughter. Like a proud dad who carries a picture of his daughter, I carried the image of you in My eyes. Before the beginning of time, I chose you. I spoke your name into the heavens, and I smiled.

You are Mine. My love for you extends farther than the stars in the sky and deeper than any ocean. You are My pearl of great price, the one for whom I gave everything. I love you even when you fail. Nothing you say can make Me stop loving you.

I want to spend time with you. I wait for you. I want to tell you how much I treasure you. I sing over you. Holding you in the palm of my hand, I am always certain of your value and your worth. —Author's adaptation of 1 John 3:2, Isaiah 43:1, Matthew 13:46, Ephesians 1:4, Psalm 149:4, Zephaniah 3:17

God's protection and provision are unfailing. Everything you need from your dad, God offers to you. He wants to talk to you, spend time with you, and connect with the deepest part of you. His opinion of you is what's important because He is the One who created you. He sees His beauty in you (Galatians 4:6-7).

A girl who understands true beauty finds her value in her

GOD'S WORD SAYS

Now that we are his children, God has sent the Spirit of his Son into our hearts. And his Spirit tells us that God is our Father. You are no longer slaves. You are God's children, and you will be given what he has promised.
—Galatians 4:6-7 CONTEMPORARY ENGLISH VERSION

Father's eyes. She finds her belonging in Him. She sees His heart of love for her. After all, she is His daughter, the beauty of His eyes.

Looking in the Mirror

1. On a scale of 1 to 10 (1 being the weakest, 10 being the strongest), how strong is your relationship with your dad?

2. In what ways do you see your dad's protection—or lack of protection—in your life?

3. How has your relationship with your dad shaped how you view yourself?

4. Identify areas where you need to forgive your dad.

5. What images come to mind when you think of God being your Father?

6. In what way has your view of God as your Father been shaped by your relationship with your earthly father?

7. Do you believe that God sees you as His beautiful daughter? Why or why not?

8. What do you look like through the Father's eyes? Be specific.

Keep me as the apple of your eye;

hide me in the shadow of your wings.

−Psalm 17:8

..........9

DESIGNED BY GOD

WHEN God began healing my faulty understanding of beauty, I hoped I'd never again struggle to understand my worth. I wanted to wake up every morning and be absolutely thrilled with the person looking back at me from the mirror.

But I had another startling discovery to make. Walking in His beauty is not an event; it's a life-long process. We don't get up one day and never again hear the critical voices, feel the temptation to use our bodies for attention, or wonder if we're beautiful.

We live in a world that presses in close on every side as it shouts for our attention. We still see the same perfect bodies staring at us from magazine racks and billboards, we still face the dressing room mirrors when buying clothes, and we still live in a very broken world.

Days will come when you will wake up and wonder if who you are is good enough. Some days you may question whether or not you are truly beautiful. And you will have days when you think it would be easier to put the mask back on and forget being the real you.

The important thing isn't that these questions and doubts return but that you learn how to respond to them. Each day you must choose to see yourself through God's eyes.

When your body began changing from that of a little girl into a young woman, you didn't wake up one morning with two full-sized breasts and fully developed hips. Becoming a woman is a process, and so is coming to understand God's beauty in us and His purpose for us.

Too many times we want God to just slap on spiritual change so we can avoid the hard work of growing in our relationship with Him. But that's not how life works. To grow in His beauty, we have to nourish our relationship with Him. Our choices will either hinder or encourage spiritual growth.

GOD'S WORD SAYS

~~~~~~~~~~

For the sinful nature desires what is contrary to the Spirit, and the Spirit what is contrary to the sinful nature. They are in conflict with each other, so that you do not do what you want. But if you are led by the Spirit, you are not under law. —Galatians 5:17-18

Our flesh and God's Spirit are at war with one another (Galatians 5:17-18). Satan wants us to feel worthless, so he keeps urging us to give in to the desires of our flesh. The resulting self-hatred is an indication that we are living by the flesh.

Living by the Spirit keeps us from compromising who we were created to be.

Transforming the Mind

The mind is powerful and its cooperation is crucial. To understand our God-given beauty we must change our minds, but old thoughts don't give up without a struggle. The Bible says that we can resist the world by renewing our minds (Romans 12:2; Ephesians 4:23-24).

Transforming our minds is much more than just thinking good thoughts. The word *renew* means to make something old new again. God created us with minds that reflect His design for beauty, but our minds have become infected with the world's way of thinking. When we make the choice to love God above all else, He changes the desires of our hearts. Our minds, however, continue to think like the world until we allow the Holy Spirit to teach us how to think like Christ. Just as God can change the desires of our hearts, He can also change the way we think.

THE WORLD SAYS

- Doing whatever you want will make you feel strong.

- Saying whatever is on your mind will make you feel important.

GOD'S WORD SAYS

Do not conform any longer to the pattern of this world, but be transformed by the renewing of your mind. Then you will be able to test and approve what God's will is—his good, pleasing and perfect will. —Romans 12:2

[You are] to be made new in the attitude of your minds; and to put on the new self, created to be like God in true righteousness and holiness. —Ephesians 4:23-24

If we allow Him room to work, the Holy Spirit will show us which thoughts are godly and which are worldly (Romans 8:5).

To live in agreement with the Spirit we must *set* our minds on the Spirit. If we "set" something on its course, we determine the direction it will go. The same is true with our minds. If we "set" our minds on the Spirit, we turn our thoughts in the direction of the Holy Spirit.

The word *set* is used to convey another idea. If we make something out of clay and allow it to "set," it will harden into the shape we have formed. When we "set" our minds on the Spirit, our thoughts will harden in the shape of God's thoughts. Our thinking will be formed to fit the shape of God's desires.

When we allow the Holy Spirit to direct us, He steers us away from thoughts that are contrary to the truth of God's Word. When we're dealing with thoughts that don't reflect God's truth, we have to choose to remove them from our minds. Simply put, any thought that doesn't line up with the Word of God has to go. This takes practice, but with God's help it can be done (2 Corinthians 10:5).

Our thoughts determine our actions. If we center our thoughts on what the world says about beauty, we will try to look like the world. However, if we center our thoughts on what God says about beauty, we begin to show the beauty of Christ.

We must *choose* to let go of the world's definition of beauty. We must *choose* to see ourselves as God sees us. We must *choose* to invest in things that have eternal spiritual value.

When you look at a picture of yourself what's your usual response? Do you compare yourself to others in the picture or to some idealized image of what you wish you looked like? If you feel as if you don't measure up, you may frown, groan, or even go so far as to cut yourself out of the picture.

But when our mind has been changed by the Holy Spirit, we're able to look at ourselves without cringing. We see ourselves as a unique expression of a loving God. Our minds filter the voices we hear and listen only to those that are good (Philippians 4:8).

Sometimes we need to hear constructive criticism from those trying to help us, but listening to words of failure, rejection, and inadequacy will destroy the young woman you were created to be. The voices you listen to must agree with what you "hear" from the Word of God. If they don't, you must stop letting them into your mind.

Part of the process of renewing our minds is recognizing Satan's lies. We can identify his words because he speaks words of rejection, failure, and discontent. He says things like . . .

"You'll never measure up."

"You're so fat."

GOD'S WORD SAYS

Summing it all up, friends, I'd say you'll do best by filling your minds and meditating on things true, noble, reputable, authentic, compelling, gracious—the best, not the worst; the beautiful, not the ugly; things to praise, not things to curse. —Philippians 4:8
THE MESSAGE

"You're a failure."

"If you were thinner, people would want to hang out with you more."

"You'll never be as beautiful as she is."

"You can't even pick the right outfit to wear."

"Your hair looks stupid."

"You are not good at anything."

"Your breasts are too small."

"No one wants to be around you."

"Your hips are too big."

"You are so ugly."

He even tries to convince us that God doesn't really care about us.

"If God really cared, He wouldn't have made you look this way."

"If you can't believe God loves you just the way you are, His love must not be true."

"If you were really spiritual, you wouldn't struggle to love yourself."

GOD'S WORD SAYS

Turn to my reproof, behold, I will pour out my spirit on you; I will make my words known to you. —Proverbs 1:23

NASB

Lies. All lies. When we expose them, they lose their power because we no longer believe them and act accordingly (Proverbs 1:23).

The word *turn* in Proverbs 1:23 is the Hebrew word *shub*, which means "to turn back."[1] When we've been deceived by Satan's lies about ourselves and about beauty, we need to "turn back" to God's truth on the subject. We turn away from our wrong thinking and living, and toward right thinking and living.

However, we can't rely on what we *think* God says. We need to *know* what He says by reading His Word (Isaiah 55:8-9).

God's Word changes the way we think. The Holy Spirit shows us the thoughts that hold our minds and hearts in captivity. When we transfer those thoughts to the captivity of Christ, God releases us from their control.

Each time we choose to do what the Word says, our minds become more set in the ways of the Spirit.

GOD'S WORD SAYS

"For my thoughts are not your thoughts, neither are your ways my ways," declares the LORD. "As the heavens are higher than the earth, so are my ways higher than your ways and my thoughts than your thoughts." —Isaiah 55:8-9

Seeing ourselves in the mirror of God's Word rather than in the world's mirror affects our everyday decisions.

- Rather than thinking about food and exercise as a way to reach a certain size, we make choices as a way to be strong and healthy so we can accomplish what God designed us to do.

- Rather than constantly checking to make sure our hair and makeup look just right, we check to make sure our hearts are in the right place.

- Rather than worrying whether our clothes match the latest fashions, we make sure our attitudes match what God says we should believe.

- Rather than wonder if others consider us beautiful, we walk in the confidence that God is forming His beauty in us.

Living in Worship

The Gospel of Luke tells of a woman who found her true beauty. In the presence of Jesus, she did the only thing she knew to do. She worshiped Him. The unidentified woman washed His feet with her tears, dried them with her hair, and then poured expensive perfume on them (7:37-50).

Scripture doesn't tell us anything about the woman's appearance. Her height, weight, and hair color remain unknown. We know only that she came to worship the One who loved her. And she did so with planned extravagance. When the homeowner recognized her, he was surprised that Jesus would allow such a sinful woman to touch Him. But the man's opinion didn't stop her. The only opinion that mattered to her was that of Jesus.

Fear keeps us from doing a lot of things. We hold back from making new friendships because we're afraid we might be rejected. We don't try new things because we're afraid we might look silly. And we don't live out our dreams because we're afraid we might fail.

But true worshipers don't worry about what others think of them. Worshipers are free to be the person God made them to be. As a worshiper, my whole life becomes a work of His beauty, a life lived *wholly* unto Him. This means that everything I do, I do for Him (Colossians 3:23-24; 2 Corinthians 5:14-15).

My life is not mine. If Christ lives in me, my life will express the love of Christ to others. It's the same with my beauty. If my beauty comes from knowing that I am fearfully and wonderfully made by a loving God, my beauty will bring attention to Him, not to me. Simply put, my beauty should tell the story of what God has done in my life.

Godly beauty says, "In Christ I have found the greatest love I've ever known, and I want my life to give that same hope to others."

When the apostle Paul wrote to Timothy about proper dress for women, he was not condemning women for doing their hair or wearing jewelry. He was simply saying that true beauty comes from being a woman of God, not from fitting in with popular fads and fashions (1 Timothy 2:9-10).

When we pursue the beauty

THE WORLD SAYS

I need to look a certain way, so I can get others to look at me. That will fill the emptiness I feel.

GOD'S WORD SAYS

And I want women to get in there with the men in humility before God, not primping before a mirror or chasing the latest fashions but *doing something beautiful for God and becoming beautiful doing it.* —1 Timothy 2:9-10 THE MESSAGE, emphasis added that comes from God, not only will we be filled with the beauty of Christ, but that beauty will begin pouring out from us. When the woman poured perfume on Jesus' feet, fragrance filled the room. In the same way, when our lives contain the beauty God designed for us, it will spill out into every area of our lives—including our desires, personality, and physical appearance—so that those around us will become aware of the beauty of Christ.

Walking down the hallway with its pale blue walls and well-worn linoleum, she is vaguely aware of her surroundings. She hears the laughter carrying from one group of friends to another, but their chatter remains distant as she listens to the voice of another. Quiet yet clear, she hears Him gently call, "Hello, My love. You are beautiful."

A smile softly spreads across her face as she feels the full warmth of His presence. She feels loved. She feels safe. She feels chosen.

Making her way to her locker, she opens it and begins her morning ritual of emptying her backpack of its burdens only to fill it again with the books and assignments she will need for her classes. When she looks up, the eyes of the girl at the next locker catch her attention. She remembers the look all too well—empty, hurt, alone, but hiding behind the look of perfection.

Hungering for the approval of others, she spent many days in brokenness, her true beauty hidden behind the mask. She struggled to hold herself together with a smile that lied. Always trying harder, always wishing life were different, continually striving to be different by looking different. And then He found her.

Picking her up from the ground where she lay overcome by her tears, He cradled her in His arms, held her close, and sang love songs to her.

The harsh sound of the warning bell reverberates in her ears as she reaches into her purse to take out the necklace and earrings she grabbed off her dresser in her hurry to get to school. She puts them on, adjusts her shirt and jeans, and takes one last look in the mirror.

Finally understanding her own great worth, she no longer needs the approval of others. She has seen into the eyes of her Creator and has found a place of belonging that she never imagined. No longer driven by the expectations of others, she rejoices in the great freedom she has found in loving Him.

She is beautiful.

She is you.

Slamming her locker door shut and turning to face her day, she catches the other girl's eyes. *Tell her*, she hears Him say.

"I will," she says. "I certainly will."

Looking in the Mirror

1. Following the Holy Spirit is a daily discipline. In what ways should you "put on the new self, which is being renewed in knowledge in the image of its Creator" (Colossians 3:10)?

2. List some of the lies the enemy has tried to make you believe. Using your Bible (and a concordance if you have one), find a Scripture and write it down to answer each accusation.

3. The words of John's Revelation say, "Those whom I love I rebuke and discipline. So be earnest, and repent" (3:19). In this verse, the Greek word for *repent* is *metanoeo,* which means "to think differently."[2] What are some ways you need to accept the Lord's correction and choose to "think differently" about yourself?

4. Read the following verses: 1 Chronicles 16:29, Psalm 27:4, Psalm 29:2, Psalm 96:6. What do these Scriptures teach about the connection between a life of beauty and a life of worship?

5. Read 2 Corinthians 2:14-15. In what ways can your life be a sweet fragrance?

May you walk confidently in His beauty as you remember . . .

The Lord your God is with you, he is mighty to save. He will
take great delight in you, he will quiet you with his love,
he will rejoice over you with singing.

–Zephaniah 3:17

NOTES

Chapter 1—Beauty and the Deception

1. *Seventeen*, August 2005, 22.

2. *Seventeen*, September 2005, 23.

3. *Seventeen*, September 2005, 23.

4. *Teen Vogue*, February 2005, 18.

5. Aeropostale advertisement, *Seventeen*, September 2005, 58-59.

6. Cover-Girl advertisement, *CosmoGIRL!*, September 2005, 7.

7. *Seventeen*, September 2005, 23.

8. Ibid.

9. *Seventeen*, August 2005, 21.

10. *Seventeen*, August 2005, 21.

11. Brilliant Brunette by John Frieda advertisement, *Seventeen*, August 2005, 138-139.

Chapter 2—Voices All Around

1. Talea Santiago, et al, "Get a Grip," *The Augusta Chronicle*, May 31, 2005, 9-10A.

2. Ibid.

Chapter 3—True Beauty

1. "Sanctuary." *Webster's Ninth New Collegiate Dictionary*. Springfield: Merriam-Webster, 1989. 1040.

2. "Thuo." *e-sword. Thayer's Greek Dictionary*. 2380.

Chapter 4—A Modest Appeal

1. Dannah Gresh, *Secret Keeper: The Delicate Power of Modesty* (Chicago: Moody Press, 2002), 38.

2. Ibid., 43.

3. Stephen Arterburn, Fred Stoeker, and Mike Yorkey, *Every Young Man's Battle: Strategies for Victory in the Real World of Sexual Temptation* (Colorado Springs: WaterBrook Press, 2002), 56-57, 78.

4. "Discretion," *Webster's Ninth New Collegiate Dictionary*, 1989 ed.

Chapter 9—Designed by God

1. "Shub." *e-sword. Strong's Concordance*. H7725.

2. "Metanoeo." *e-sword. Strong's Concordance*. G3340.

Note to the Reader

The publisher invites you to share your response to
the message of this book by writing Discovery House
Publishers, Box 3566, Grand Rapids, MI 49501, USA. For
information about other Discovery House books, music, or
videos, contact us at the same address or call 1-800-653-
8333. Find us on the Internet at http://www.dhp.org/ or
send e-mail to books@dhp.org.